THE ADVENTURE

Putting Energy into Your Walk with God

JERRY SITTSER

Foreword by Leighton Ford

INTERVARSITY PRESS
DOWNERS GROVE, ILLINOIS 60515

InterVarsity Press is the book-publishing division of Inter-Varsity Christian Fellowship, a student movement active on campus at hundreds of universities, colleges and schools of nursing in the United States of America, and a member movement of the International Fellowship of Evangelical Students. For information about local and regional activities, write Public Relations Dept., InterVarsity Christian Fellowship, 6400 Schroeder Rd., P.O. Box 7895, Madison, WI 53707-7895.

All quotations from Scripture, unless otherwise noted, are from the Revised Standard Version of the Bible, copyrighted 1946, 1952, © 1971, 1973 by the Division of Christian Education of the National Council of the Churches of Christ in the U.S.A., and used by permission.

The quotation on page 198 is taken from Notes to Myself by Hugh Prather © 1970 Real People Press and is used by permission.

The stanza on page 51 is from "Great Is Thy Faithfulness" by Thomas O. Chisholm. Copyright 1923. Renewal 1951 by Hope Publishing Co., Carol Stream, IL 60188. Used by permission.

Cover illustration: Greg Wray

ISBN 0-87784-335-X

Printed in the United States of America

Library of Congress Cataloging in Publication Data
Sittser, Jerry, 1950-
    The adventure: putting energy into your walk with God.

    Bibliography: p.
      1. Christian life—1960   I. Title.
BV4501.2.S4734   1985   248.4   85-19695
ISBN 0-87784-335-X

17   16   15   14   13   12   11   10   9   8
04

To my mother, Grace,
whose name
so perfectly describes
her character.

Foreword

Christianity's biggest problem in modern America has not been underexposure. Quite the opposite. Dozens of TV shows, scores of seminars and hundreds of books and articles have highlighted the "born-again movement."

The biggest problem in my judgment has been overexposure of a diluted gospel—a gospel offering health, wealth and success without the power to change people from the kingdom of self into the kingdom of God. That kind of exposure inoculates people against the true way of Christ.

The greatest evangelistic impact today would be for people to see followers of Jesus Christ living the life of the kingdom. As an acquaintance of mine said with some surprise about a neighbor, "She is the first *Christian* Christian I've met."

This is why I regard *The Adventure* as a significant book. Its theme is vital. Not once, to my knowledge, does the New Testament speak of "accepting Christ as Savior." Certainly he is our only Savior. Surely he must be trusted. But the biblical writer speaks instead of "receiving Christ as *Lord*" and "continuing to *live* in him" (Col 2:6). Life in and under the King is what knowing Christ is all about.

Jerry Sittser compels us to explore the new life. He writes biblically, theologically, practically and interestingly. In an age that either discards discipleship or makes it a virtuoso performance, he shows the exciting adventure of responding to what God is doing in our lives, in his church and in history.

In this book I found hope. Jerry Sittser is one of the many emerging young leaders who dares to reach out for God's new work. It makes me want to join Jerry and the Sage in being part of the Adventure!

Leighton Ford
Charlotte, North Carolina
July 1985

Preface

I am a chaplain at a Christian liberal arts college. When I arrived at the campus in the fall of 1979, I quickly observed two characteristics of our students. First, they had many misconceptions of the Christian faith. They tended to attach themselves to one attractive part of Christianity (for instance, the charismatic movement or ascetic spirituality) and then reduce the whole of the Christian faith to that one part. Sooner or later this resulted in either self-righteousness or disillusionment, depending on whether their reductionism worked. Second, they lacked motivation. The Christian life was parenthetical to their lives. It required only a small commitment of time, belief in a set of innocuous religious ideas, a posture of politeness and ownership of a heavenly insurance policy. It was not a way of life for most students.

I also learned that it was not much more than that for me. So I set out to explore the Christian life as a whole—its many parts logically and necessarily connected together. I also wanted to make it livable. This book, then, arose from biblical study and practical ministry. It is a reflection of my work with students, who helped shape my theology.

The opportunity to write this book came from Leighton Ford, an evangelist with the Billy Graham Association. He visited our campus in the fall of 1982 and, for no apparent reason, took an interest in me and my work. On one occasion he visited my office and skimmed a few essays I had written. Before leaving he told me that he was going to write Jim Sire, the editor at InterVarsity Press, to introduce me. Later I received a letter from IVP asking me to submit an outline of my book idea. What you have before you is the finished product.

The purpose of the book is twofold. First, I want to clarify truth. I hope to lay a foundation of simple truths that logically connect together. One of the weaknesses of American Christianity is that it takes one part of the Christian faith and makes it the whole. When that one part fails to work for us, we tend to become spiritually vulnerable and so bounce from one religious fad to the next. I hope to correct this by exploring the whole of the Christian faith, which I think is greater than the sum of its parts.

Second, I want to motivate Christians to be mature disciples. I believe that there is drama in the Christian life. It is full of wonder and power. By its very nature it will not allow us to be casual in the way we live it out. The Christian life demands commitment and promises adventure. I want readers to catch the vision. I want them to gain a sense of destiny.

The structure of the book is a logical progression. Each section has a brief introduction that explains where readers have just come from, where they will be going next and how the two sections connect together. Because I believe truth is more than mere abstraction, I have used a peculiar device to make the book more human and practical. Chapter one introduces readers to the story of my relationship with a wise old man whom I call the Sage. The rest of the chapters all begin with brief sketches of the experiences and conversations I had with him. Each sketch somehow introduces the content of the chapter, mostly through analogies or illustrations.

The Sage, I must confess, is not a real person. I did grow up in Western Michigan, as chapter one explains. And my parents did have a cottage on Lake Michigan. My grandfather even had a cabin on the lake, one roughly similar to the Sage's. The Sage is perhaps a portrait of what I wanted my grandfather to be and what I want to be for my grandchildren someday. The character of the Sage is molded after three people: a former colleague at the college, a pastor in my denomination and an uncle who died while I was in college. The first of these three men showed me extraordinary kindness and humility; the second taught me loyalty and wisdom; the third—a poet, doctor and thinker—encouraged me to become sensitive to life. These men have all been sages to me.

The sketches are mostly true. They either happened as recorded, happened in different circumstances or happened to someone else. The most unbelievable of them, chapter ten, is true as recorded, except that the narrator was in a PT boat and not an airplane. The final sketch is my invention. No one I know has ever received such a letter.

I hope this book will impart a vision. It is obviously not the final word on discipleship. At best, it is only an introduction to a new way of seeing life—as something wonderful, full of mystery and power, and, ultimately, glory. Like the seed that grows into a mighty oak, we are now in the process of dying to the old and growing up into something we hardly dare even imagine. I hope this book pushes all of us a little closer to the goal.

Acknowledgments

As in all projects, both great and small, what one person does is usually the product of the contributions of many people. It is unfortunate that only one name must appear on the front cover. I want to acknowledge the many people to whom I am indebted. First, three persons from InterVarsity Press deserve special mention: Joan Lloyd Guest, Michael Maudlin and James Sire. All three took the risk to invest time and money in me when I showed little evidence of being worthy of it. I am also indebted to the students at Northwestern College who endured my teaching and challenged me to become more theologically precise and more practical. Further, I want to thank several people who read and critiqued earlier drafts, among them Ron Nelson, Nella Kennedy, Barney Hamady, David Bast, David Myers, Judy Koerselman, Jack Veltkamp, Kevin Korver, Steve Thulson and Lynn Cheyney. I am grateful for their investment of time and energy. My wife, Lynda Sittser, was very kind and encouraging through the whole process. Finally, I am indebted to Linda Schulte, who typed and corrected many drafts. She was always kind, diligent and accurate.

I
MAKING SENSE
OUT OF
DISCIPLESHIP

A teen-ager's encounter with a remarkable old man introduces us to the scheme of the book, which is to tell the story of a human relationship and to explore the wisdom toward which it points. Such wisdom begins when we understand that the Christian faith, so often reduced to the simplistic and popular, is actually comprehensive. It has many dimensions that, when brought together, create a perfect whole. Discipleship is the process of learning about and experiencing this wholeness.

Chapter 1

SUMMER
WITH THE SAGE

EVERY SUMMER WHILE I was growing up my family used to vacation for a couple of months at a small cottage toward the northern end of Lake Michigan. We were secluded there. The lake was cold, the beach stony, the weather unpredictable, so the area was not very popular. Also, the people who traveled to the north were very private. They wanted nothing to do with water-skiing, golf and deck parties at dusk. They were not the kind to roam around yacht clubs and dine at fancy restaurants. They relished solitude.

Down the way from us lived a couple of brothers, retired, I think, whose wives had died on the same day in 1963. I only saw them early in the morning, when they would launch their boat to go fishing. They always returned promptly at 10:00 A.M., never to be seen for the rest of the day. My mom once took them some cookies, which they received politely. But they always kept their distance. A friend told me their wives were buried together in a plot next to their cabin, and they sat right over the graves every afternoon in total silence. I never really believed this story, but what he said was enough to keep me away.

Just north of us lived a painter and her bearded husband, who earned his living as a weaver and potter. My dad often poked fun at them, calling them "hippies." During my years in junior high, I usually visited them twice a week. Edward always showed me his new pots and rugs, and Rachel served me a snack. They made me feel grown-up. My parents, however, disapproved of these visits because Edward and Rachel were only "pretending" to be married and were therefore a bad influence on me. I never thought much about that. I was more interested in the food. Besides, they said I was their favorite guest.

I'm ashamed to say now that in the spring I always complained about our yearly migration. My friends teased me about going away with my parents for the summer, as if that were the ultimate blow to my quest for independence. I thought then that I would miss the freedom of spending hours every day swimming in friends' pools, riding bicycles and sitting in the local McDonald's drinking Coke and eating french fries slower than a connoisseur tastes a new wine. As I look back, I think I felt obligated to grumble about these summer vacations. I gained respectability by balking at my parents' plans. But I know now that I secretly welcomed the yearly sojourn and was relieved to escape the pressure and boredom of being with my friends every day.

During my high-school years I worked at a gas station in town. There I learned about small-town culture and people, both of which intrigued me, if for no other reason than that they were so different from me. I became fast friends with the local sheriff, the town drunk and a fellow gas pumper and mechanic who claimed to know the Volkswagen engine better than its inventor. I almost believed that he had grease instead of blood running through his veins.

My last summer at the cottage, however, proved to be the most significant, for I met and came to know a wise and weathered man whom I now call the Sage. The year was 1971, and I was about to begin my freshman year in college. I can't quite remember how I first heard about him. I think my sister saw him one afternoon while she was walking down one of the many dirt roads in the woods. But she couldn't remember much about him. My mom said she had heard about him at the local grocery store. He was new to the area, she said; he was a private sort of man who minded his own business and invited everyone else to mind his business, too. A couple of days later my dad met him on the beach. My dad said he was polite but distant. I suggested that we all go to visit him. But my mother decided, all too undemocratically, that we should leave him alone.

It was, however, already too late for that. I was too curious to pass up meeting such a mysterious man. So I kept my eyes open for some sign of him and my ears tuned to the gossip that began spreading like a contagious disease. New people always drew the attention of the local townspeople, who resented the invasions of strangers. At the gas station I heard from a local real estate agent that he was from New York and, though married once, was now living alone. She had been a famous singer on the East Coast, he a successful lawyer. I also learned that he was at one time wealthy but had more recently been living in relative poverty. Someone mentioned that he might have lost all his money betting on horses. I discovered that he was something of a hermit who supposedly shunned visitors.

"Is he hiding something?" I asked the town barber.

"Probably," he said.

I wondered what it could be, and who he could be.

About a week later I finally saw him at a distance as he peddled his bicycle by the station. I could discern no details, except for the color of his clothing (blue) and the color of his hair (white). I decided that I simply must meet this man. I planned to pay him a visit.

I learned that he lived on the lake, so the next week I meandered a half mile through the woods until I found his cabin. Feeling untypically self-conscious, as if I were spying on him, I looked around carefully to stake the place out. Then I walked up until I was perhaps twenty yards from his front porch.

His cabin was well kept. A rocker sat on his front porch. Next to it a table held a few dishes and a couple of thick books. Leaning against the wall was a fishing pole, with a tackle box right underneath. There were some plants hanging from the beams of the porch and flower boxes underneath both front windows. On the door hung a sign that read, "Welcome." About ten yards away a hammock was strung between two large birch trees. Near it grew a large garden of beans, carrots, lettuce, peas and other vegetables. Guarding the corners of his front lawn stood birdhouses and feeders which were, by the sight and sound of it, doing their job quite well. At the end of the lawn a flight of redwood stairs led down to the beach.

The place was too friendly to study at a distance. So, without further hesitation, I marched right up to the front porch and peeked into one of the windows.

"Is anybody home?" a voice said behind me.

I was too surprised to move, but too curious not to look. So I turned my head slowly to see who spoke to me and to say something—anything—that would explain what I was doing. When I saw who it was, which should have been no surprise to me, I became, for the first time in my life, speechless.

There stood the old man, staring at me. He had white hair, with wisps of it falling over his ears, a white beard and a square face, with lines carved out by smiles and important thoughts. His forehead made him look inquisitive, his eyebrows stern; but his eyes and mouth were those of a most friendly man. He appeared healthy and energetic. He was short and a little bowlegged. He wore baggy gray pants which were too short for him, a red-and-white checked shirt and suspenders. He looked a little like an unmade bed.

"I was wondering when someone was going to visit me," he said, smiling. Then he walked briskly over to me and extended his hand. "Welcome to my home."

However much I wanted to greet him, I discovered that I was unable to move. All my thoughts about this man, scattered about in my mind by the winds of my imagination, finally came to rest on the person standing before me. He was overwhelmingly real. I think that he knew I couldn't move, so he reached out to my side, grabbed my hand and shook it vigorously.

"You are my first visitor," he said, "and so I must treat you like a long lost friend. Please, come into my little cottage and have some soda and a cookie with me."

He led me proudly into his cabin. I was immediately struck by its cozy and cluttered atmosphere. It had a fireplace with a few smoldering embers from the previous night's fire and a small study with books stacked everywhere. The whole place smelled of pipe tobacco and freshly baked bread. The small kitchen boasted a cast-iron stove, pots and pans hanging from the ceiling beams, and vases of flowers set on every conceivable shelf and table.

I stayed for three hours. It seemed like we talked about everything—politics, religion, gas stations, the weather and ourselves. That first encounter, so memorable in itself, led to a rich relationship with a man whose life, so full of struggle and drama, had led him not to bitterness and selfishness, but to wisdom and character. My summer with him awakened me to a seasoned and sober view of life. I am forever endebted to him.

I want to tell the story of our friendship. But I also want to say something more: I want to tell you about the kind of life toward which our friendship pointed me. So, using snapshots of the summer—stories he told me, conversations we had, issues we discussed and experiences we shared—I wish to impart something of the spirit of his life and the truth he believed in. The Sage was a Christian man, thoroughly and naturally. He influenced me most by introducing me to the wonder and rigor of the Christian life. That is what I hope to do for you.

Chapter 2

GETTING
THE BIGGER
PICTURE

I SOON LEARNED THAT the Sage was a good storyteller. I still remember the first story he ever told me. It was about two weeks after we met. We were discussing my church and how bored I felt whenever I attended. My religion stifled me. He listened patiently, and then he told this story:

"Once there was a kind old king who lived in a great castle overlooking a city. His wife had died when young, without bearing any children. Since he had never found another to equal her, he lived all alone.

"One day he decided to adopt some children with whom he could share his wealth and among whom he could divide his kingdom. This would ensure that his throne would be passed on to those most prepared to assume it. He introduced the idea to his wizards and counselors, and they all agreed that it was a splendid idea. They suggested he look for the very best blood in the land from which to select his children. This was wise counsel, he thought; but after a night of sleepless reflection he determined that the honor should go to the most undeserving. So he sent a delegation to an orphanage in the city to find four children, two boys and two girls. Soon his castle was filled with the sounds of gleeful children and was bustling with their wide-eyed activities.

"How the king loved them. Being alone for so long, he had stored up a huge surplus of affection and kindness which he lavished on them. He played with them every day. He read books to them, mostly accounts of his earlier exploits against dragons and invading armies. He taught them the rudimentary skills of kingship. He held them on his lap a great deal too. While everyone in the court called him 'Your Highness' or 'Great King' or 'My Lord,' his children called him 'Daddy.' That pleased him more than anything.

"Since the king expected that they would someday rule over the four states of his kingdom, he made their training rigorous and thorough. Every morning they arose at 6:30 A.M. for exercise. At 7:00 they ate a hearty breakfast. Then for the rest of the morning they studied with the grand wizard. They learned the ways of animals and insects, the complexity of flowers and trees, the techniques of alchemy, the rules of war and peace, court manners, science and mathematics, and much more. In the afternoons they practiced using the bow, sword and catapult. They learned how to hunt with falcons, how to stalk prey and how to sing ballads and write poetry. Finally, in the evening they listened to the king tell stories, or they strolled through the woods or down the city streets, where they greeted the common people and listened to their needs.

"As the children grew up, however, each began very subtly to grow proud. They started to spend more time pursuing what was to them pleasant and natural and avoiding what they considered toilsome. The oldest of the four, Henry, passed his hours in the castle library, where he read books on magic, the arts and kingship. He became a man of extraordinary knowledge, but he grew to hate exercise and even polite conversation.

"Elizabeth, the next in line, relished the wealth and finery of the castle. She rode the royal horses, ate the royal food and spent the royal money. Every evening she dressed up in ostentatious gowns and paraded around the castle. She talked constantly and gossiped far too much, but excused these vices to her brothers and sister by saying, with a giggle, 'You're just jealous.' She despised correction and hard work, and she dodged all discipline.

"Jonathan was the disciplined one. Six in the morning was too late for him to rise. He usually sprang out of bed at 5:00 and sometimes 4:00. He ran miles every day through the royal forest. He practiced using the bow and sword until his hands bled. He pushed himself to the limits of his strength and ability, but he became impatient, unfriendly and intolerant of others, especially if they were lazy, as Elizabeth was. Besides, he never used his training for real battles or quests.

"The youngest, Sarah, pursued too many noble causes. She was always racing out of the castle to intervene in some dispute, to defend one of the outlying towns from the advances of a malevolent force or to square off against the dragons of the north. Later, she always returned to the castle bruised, beaten and bitter. She loathed her brothers and sister for their cowardice, and they made matters worse by taunting her with her failures.

"So it happened, over time, that the king's children embraced one aspect of royal living and disregarded the rest and so became lop-sided in their interests, judgmental of the others and self-justifying. And every one of them failed. Henry gained knowledge but had no wisdom. Elizabeth enjoyed the royal privileges but became fat, lazy and vain. Jonathan disciplined himself but forgot what his regimentation was for. Sarah embraced worthy causes but never prepared herself for them or enlisted the help of others.

"The king's plan to share his authority and wealth was thwarted. He became very sad and wondered what had gone amiss."

As was usually the case, the Sage finished the story and then dismissed its value by saying something like, "Ah, just the ramblings of a dreary old man. Let's go for a walk."

*   *   *

Many Paths, One Direction

I became a Christian for a specific reason. I was morally spineless and confused about my future, so I was attracted to the Christ of the Gospels whose personal integrity made him courageous. I was also impressed by the early disciples who were able to stand firmly on their confession of Christ, even though it led to suffering. I wanted that kind of strength and character. I still do.

People have different reasons for becoming Christians, and they are usually legitimate ones. Some, for example, embrace Christianity because it offers peace of mind and confidence in life. Social pressures, job requirements, family responsibilities and global problems vex us and exhaust us. We welcome the words of Jesus, "Come to me, all you who are weary and burdened, and I will give you rest" (Mt 11:28 NIV). Jesus is our Shepherd; God is our Father. In Christianity we discover a God who accepts us for who we are. It makes us feel good about ourselves.

Others, especially those who are adventurous and energetic, find in Christianity an opportunity to pursue some lofty and arduous goal. The words of Jesus stir us to action: "follow me"; "count the cost"; "deny yourself and take up your cross." That cross, we think, is some cause—nuclear arms reduction, world hunger relief, refugee resettlement, the prolife movement, women's liberation. We join the organizations and follow the popular movements that thrust us into the heart of some religious war. In this way of thinking, Jesus is the Messiah; God is our King; and the world is a battlefield.

Still others are moved by the discipline Christianity requires. Perhaps we are naturally disciplined, like an athlete or a musician, and so Christianity appeals to this propensity. Or we might be just the opposite, and Christianity pushes us to cultivate needed habits. In either case, we immerse ourselves in study, prayer, fasting and other spiritual disciplines. Jesus becomes like a drill sergeant. We are serious about such verses as, "Train yourself in godliness," and "Run the race with endurance."

Then there are those who adopt the Christianity of certain success. Either we are already successful and we want a religion that affirms that, or we are fed up with failure and are looking for a way out. We like the gospel of health and wealth and positive thinking. Verses promising prosperity, fruitfulness and abundance compel us. We follow religious television and attend "dynamic" and "growing" churches. We wallow in the luxury of being one of God's chosen people.

Some of us were born and raised as Christians. Weekly church attendance and knowledge of Christian doctrines are second nature to us. We are products of a Christian home and children of the covenant. We cannot remember a time when we did not know Jesus as Savior, and we cannot imagine losing our faith now or in the future. It is rooted in our very constitutions and sustained by an ongoing participation in the denomination that nurtured us to maturity.

None of these reasons for becoming a Christian are wrong. The Christian faith obviously calls us to uphold noble causes; it offers us peace and confidence; it requires discipline; it promises prosperity—it does all this and more. These are all legitimate paths that lead us into the heart of the gospel. And all of us, if we are Christian, have traveled one of them.

Going the Distance

But being followers of Jesus Christ requires and promises more. The paths just mentioned are important dimensions of Christianity, but the whole is greater. Christianity is by definition comprehensive; it envelops all of life. Our understanding of it must expand until it reaches the dimensions of the biblical design.

If our faith does not grow, we will give our attention to the more appealing parts of the Christian faith and neglect the rest. We will whittle it down to a more manageable size, creating a false model of discipleship, just as the four children in the Sage's story reduced their training to what appealed to their immediate interests. Our Christianity will become lopsided. We will fight God's battles without learning to rest in him and thus exhaust ourselves and perhaps become cynical. We will discipline ourselves to maturity but never be enfolded by grace and so become rigid and self-righteous. We will be healed of our problems but rarely accept the cureless pain of helping others. Or we will climb the mountain of financial, spiritual and popular success but refuse to descend into the pit of defeat, where most people live.

Suppose you just bought a new, furnished house and you are about to enter it for the first time. Obviously there are many ways to get in: through the front door, back door, porch, windows or balcony. Let's say you stroll into the house through the back door and find yourself in the kitchen. Since you are hungry, you build yourself a giant sandwich and devour it. Then you take a nap, only to wake up in time to prepare for dinner. You settle into the kitchen and gradually forget about the rest of the house.

Or let's say you slip into the library through the French doors and spy a favorite book on the shelf. You snuggle into a high-backed leather chair and begin to read. Soon you are so settled in that chair that you never want to get up.

Let's say you enter through the patio and discover the game room. Right in the middle is a pool table; so you grab a cue, chalk up and start to play a game of eight ball. In each case you rather innocently wander into one of the many rooms of the house, where you are diverted by some interest. And sadly, and not so innocently, there you stay. The house, however large it is, becomes as big as that one room; your world becomes as small; and your life becomes as lopsided—all food, all reading or all games.

The Road to Ruin

There is danger in this. Lack of a larger vision of discipleship can lead to one of two problems. First, it can make our view of the Christian life reductionistic and thus make us self-righteous. Any overattention to one aspect of Christian doctrine or experience can create imbalance and lead to a distortion of the truth. Examples of such reductionism and self-righteousness abound in the church. Some fundamentalists, for example, reduce Christian morality to conservative politics. Some mainline leaders do the same thing—only they identify Christian morality with the political left instead. Some charismatics reduce Christian experience to being filled with the Holy Spirit. Christian self-help wizards make self-esteem the key to a healthy life. Prosperity teachers reduce the gospel to the quest for health and wealth. And in each of these cases, perverted logic and imbalanced teaching make the defense of their positions almost impenetrable.

I've been guilty of this error. I remember how inflexibly dedicated I was to discipline. Of course discipline is necessary for discipleship. But my problem was that I had reduced Christianity to nothing more than certain spiritual practices. My religion was as good as my quiet time. If I missed a day, which was rare, I felt miserable. If my friends missed a few days, I doubted their devotion and treated them as inferior Christians.

In time I became a casualty of my own discipline. My efforts superseded God's grace; discipline became an obsession. To succeed in Christianity and sustain my sense of superiority over others, I constantly had to increase the rigor. Soon I was neglecting to do my chores at home, alienating myself from my wife and friends, and worshiping the Bible instead of Jesus.

That is exactly what happens when we reduce discipleship to only one dimension. We become victims of our own self-righteousness and prisoners to truncated religion. Ironically, when spiritual success becomes everything, it drives us to ruin. Once discipline is exalted, it consumes us. If service becomes the essence of Christianity, it tires us out. Reductionism and self-righteousness lead to spiritual bankruptcy.

This problem is hardly new. There are many biblical examples. Christ's disciples called him the Messiah but defined the title in self-serving ways. They wanted power, status and political independence. It took Jesus three years to teach them the truth about himself. Whenever he mentioned his true identity, therefore, it was always in the light of his imminent suffering and death (Mk 10:32-45).

On one occasion he had to rebuke Peter because he refused to see the obvious implications of Christ's calling. "Get behind me, Satan! For you are not on the side of God, but of men" (Mk 8:33). Peter thought he could muscle the kingdom of God into existence. So he boasted that he would be true to Jesus even if the others deserted. But when Jesus submitted himself to the brutal will of the Sanhedrin and centurions, Peter's spine melted. He realized that he could not war his way to greatness, that discipleship required him to be a servant.

Jesus battled the Pharisees over the same issue. They upheld the Law, a necessary element of their faith, but they resisted Christ's efforts to enlarge their view of what it meant to obey it. Jesus called them blind guides who strained at a gnat but swallowed a camel. He warned the crowds to beware of these religious leaders who could gerrymander their way out of true obedience and still be convinced that they were honoring God.

The people also resisted discipleship. They brought to Jesus their wounds and burdens, and he healed and comforted them. But he did not stop there. He never does, of course. He commanded them to be obedient, but they refused to budge. "After this many of his disciples drew back and no longer went about with him" (Jn 6:66). Jesus became unpopular because his view of discipleship was too comprehensive. He did not play into the prejudices of any one party. There was a symmetry to his thought and action. Love and judgment, obedience and power, success and suffering were all woven together.

Chasing after the Wind

The second danger of a limited vision of discipleship is to make us disillusioned and vulnerable. This is a common problem among Americans, in particular, who are so eager to find quick solutions and easy answers to complex spiritual problems. Many people make a commitment to Christ because they have a need Christ promises to meet. They hear some version of the Christian faith that guarantees fast relief. Though they feel wonderful for a while, they eventually face some problem that their limited understanding and experience cannot help them with. Then their faith, which promised to be so immediately helpful, appears to fall short. They are *not* healed, though they thought they had enough faith to be. They are *not* successful, though they applied all the self-help principles. They do *not* find peace, though they practiced meditation for months. So they become disillusioned with the religion they were told was foolproof, the final answer.

They also become vulnerable, starved for answers, and therefore baited to swallow any new religious promise. They wander into a Christian bookstore and buy the latest best seller that guarantees renewal "in five easy steps." They attend seminars in order to have their faith strengthened, marriage revived or money multiplied. In their desperation they become vulnerable to quick fixes, cheap answers and demagogic leadership, because they long to feel the heartbeat of Christianity push the blood of life through their veins.

Not that there is anything wrong with new books and "how to" seminars. But disillusioned Christians, lacking a comprehensive vision of life in Christ and the patience to go through the slow process of maturing, are easy prey to ideas and leaders who are reductionistic and ultimately heretical. Christianity in America has spawned a generation of people who appear to be willing to follow almost anyone and believe almost anything. Even cults are made up largely of sincere, albeit disillusioned, people who lack stability and balance.

The apostle Paul warned that if we fail to understand and progress toward the goal of true maturity, we will become like "children, tossed to and fro and carried about with every wind of doctrine, by the cunning of men" (Eph 4:14). Uninformed and impatient Christians end up being vulnerable.

Hope
What must we do to protect ourselves from reductionism and dis-

illusionment? First, we must understand that there is a wholeness to the Christian faith and Christian experience. Christianity is more comprehensive than we might at first be inclined to think. Discipleship is simply the process of understanding and experiencing this wholeness. It is the process of learning about the implications of Christ's lordship over all of life and applying what we learn. This means that we must strive to explore *all the dimensions* of the Christian faith until our experience becomes as multidimensional and balanced as Christ intended and the Bible teaches.

Second, we must be patient. The process of discipleship is both as simple as belonging to a family and as complex as growing up. It takes time. Although there is a direction (Part 3), it is not always an easy one. Although there is power (Part 4), it is not always self-inflating. Although there are practical dimensions (Part 6), they are not always immediately helpful. The goal of this book is simply to introduce you to the wholeness of the Christian life and to challenge you to be engaged in the process of becoming mature disciples.

Study Questions

1. For what reason did you become a Christian?
2. Are there any ways in which you have limited Christianity to only part of the truth?
3. In Matthew 23:1-36 what does Jesus teach us about self-righteousness?
4. What does Paul teach as the cure for disillusionment and vulnerability in Ephesians 4:11-16?
5. What are the marks of Christian maturity according to Matthew 5:3-12? Do you have these attributes?
6. How can we make our Christianity more whole and comprehensive?
7. Pray that God will cultivate wholeness and maturity in your life.

II
BEGINNING
WITH
GOD

Does discipleship begin with *our* commitment to God, as we are often taught, or with *God's* commitment to us? In this section we'll see that the accent of the Christian life must always be on God. The source of discipleship—where Christian living begins and where it grows—is God and not ourselves. God's loyalty to us is the foundation because it gives us security and stability in our relationship with him (chapter three). God's character creates in us a desire to know who he is (chapter four). God's pleasure, what he really desires, provides the impetus for developing true and lasting intimacy with him (chapter five). We begin, then, with another sketch from the story of the Sage to help us explore the depth of God's commitment to us.

Chapter 3

A RADICAL
COMMITMENT

FOR THE FIRST WEEKS after we met I saw the Sage almost every day. During June, since I was working afternoons and evenings at the gas station, we often used the morning to go fishing or to walk along the beach and through the woods. On my days off we cleaned his cabin, worked in his or my family's garden and talked. In fact we talked almost all the time; I learned a great deal about him. I discovered, for example, that he had been a successful lawyer in New York City but had left his practice to work with the city's poor, that he had failed as a father, and that he was going to write a book on poverty. Yet, in spite of the many questions I asked him, I always ended up talking more about myself. I gradually learned that his concern for me was sincere and extraordinary. In a week's time he seemed to know me better than I knew myself.

But the novelty of our relationship soon wore off. Being a typical teen-ager, I did not yet long for wisdom and intimacy as I do now. One day I didn't want to see him, and I don't even know why. I had a ready excuse, at least for the morning. Since I had two days off from work, my mother wanted me to scrape the deck, which I did grudgingly. But in the afternoon, although I had promised the Sage I would help him shingle his roof, I drove to a friend's house instead and spent the afternoon and part of the evening drinking beer. When I crawled out of bed the next day, I remembered what I had said to him and felt bad about it. But I soon dismissed these feelings when a friend asked if I would like to go water-skiing with his family for a day. My mother consented, although without much enthusiasm. So I packed a few things and left, not thinking at all about the Sage.

It was only after we arrived at the lake—in fact, I think I was skiing at the time—that I remembered my promise to him. I thought it silly that I should feel obligated to see the Sage and stupid that I was getting so irritated. I tried to shrug it off, but I never quite rid my mind of the strange self-consciousness I felt whenever I thought about him.

By the time I returned to our cottage I was angry. At first I tried to excuse my irritation by mentally accusing the Sage of using me to mitigate his own loneliness and helplessness. But these flimsy excuses gradually melted under the heat of my guilt, which now began to plague me. I realized I was the one who had used him. I began to see that I had made promises to him to get his attention and that I had expected far more of him than he had of me. Feeling ashamed, I didn't dare to visit him, and I assumed that he didn't want to see me either. So I began to avoid him. I started to jog south instead of north. I slept late in the mornings. And I stayed completely out of the woods, where I had often met him while he was walking. My mother noticed the change in me and casually mentioned something about it, but I snapped at her and left the room. I felt miserable.

This went on for a few days. Then, as I was running one morning along the highway, I spotted him walking slowly toward me with a sack of groceries in his arm. He was obviously immersed in thought. I considered plunging into the woods to escape his eye, but I figured he had already seen me. So I kept running toward him. As I drew near he stopped, indicating that he wanted to talk. But I increased my speed and dashed past him, greeting him only with a terse, "morning," which he returned along with a bright smile. I ran another hundred yards or so before deciding that it was immature not to stop and talk.

So I slowed down and looked back to see what he was doing. There he stood, staring right at me with a smile on his face. Of course I had committed myself by then, so I jogged back to him.

"Good morning," I said nonchalantly, acting as if I had just seen him the day before.

"I'm glad I bumped into you," he said.

"What have you been doing?" I asked.

"The same as usual. I shingled part of my roof. I cut the lawn. Oh, yes, the marigolds came up, and the roses have bloomed. Come and see."

So we walked in the direction of his cabin and fell into a friendly conversation. I forgot, for the moment, all about my anger and guilt; I also lost all sense of self-consciousness. He responded to me as if nothing had happened, as if I were a friend, a very close friend, whom he had not seen for a few days and had missed. I don't think he would ever have brought up my absence if I had not.

"I'm sorry about not visiting you for a week—I got busy I guess."

"Well," he said, "I'm glad I ran into you. I was wondering where you were."

I hesitated. "I acted kind of stupid," I said. "For a while I didn't feel like coming over, and I don't know why. So I guess I avoided you."

"I'm the same way sometimes. Don't worry about it. I welcome your visits, because I consider you a friend, like one of my grandsons whom I seldom get to see. Besides, friendship doesn't end when a person has a bad week. That's when it really begins."

I wanted to protest that he didn't understand, but I knew that I didn't have to. I realized that he did understand, even better than I did. I learned that his concern for me went deeper than my impulsiveness and immaturity and that sometimes a friendship could be carried by one person for a while, in spite of what the other did. If I was like a grandson to him, he was like a grandfather to me. I felt loved.

*   *   *

The Starting Point

In the late seventies a young college graduate, middle class and white, traveled to Southeast Asia to work with a United States refugee program. In a letter to a friend she wrote,

> There is a Franciscan Convent almost five miles from my home. I sometimes hop a bus there. The grounds are quiet and one can sit alone for hours in their chapel. As I get older, I find myself drawn to places where I can kneel and fix my eyes upon a cross. It helps my mind. I sat in the chapel last night and thought, "I hurt in so many places, on so many levels and from so many things that I cannot list or explain them; I do not pray. I am tired of hearing my mind's attempt to say something meaningful or fitting. I am just going to kneel here because I need to be healed and cleansed."[1]

That letter speaks for many of us. We, too, often hurt on so many levels and in so many places that we sometimes find it impossible to pray, worship, love, rejoice. Or believe. How can we live out the Christian faith when, for some reason, we find it almost impossible to believe in anyone, including God? What happens when faith and commitment waver?

At times the relationship between the Sage and me was one-sided. The Sage was the "carrier" of the relationship because I was, at those times, too selfish and inconsistent to contribute much to it. His example points to the foundation of the Christian faith: God's commitment to us. Our faith is grounded in God's faithfulness, his loyalty.

We know God is loyal because he has demonstrated it, first by creating the earth and establishing man as the crown of his creation. The decision to create us proves his loyalty. It was risky to make us in his image, as independent creatures. He was asking for heartache and disappointment. In a sense he was choosing, right then, to die for us.

Further, his creative action set the stage for personal investment in us, as the psalmist testifies:

I praise thee, for thou art fearful and wonderful.
    Wonderful are thy works!
Thou knowest me right well;
    my frame was not hidden from thee,
when I was being made in secret,
    intricately wrought in the depths of the earth.
Thy eyes beheld my unformed substance;
    in thy book were written, every one of them,
the days that were formed for me,
    when as yet there was none of them. (Ps 139:14-16)

Parents show the same kind of loyalty, albeit to a lesser degree. Their love for one another inspires them to love still another, a child. Ideally, it is a choice, not an obligation, to have children. That was true for my wife and me. We were married eleven years before we had our first child, a girl. We were loyal to her long before she was ever born. Our commitment to her grew throughout the pregnancy. We understood the perils. We knew that we would experience joy and agony, both the unavoidable fruits of parenthood. We were sobered, too, by the bitterness and sorrow of a close friend whose first baby was stillborn. "The choice to love requires the courage to grieve," she said.

Demonstrations of God's loyalty did not end at creation. Throughout history he has initiated a relationship with the human race, thus affirming his persistent commitment to us, even when we have been cold-hearted toward him. He called Abraham; later he formed a nation. Through that one man and that one nation he extended his loving reach to the whole world.

His loyalty rouses him even to discipline us (Heb 12:7-9) and to warn us when we do not respond. The prophets harangued against the greed and self-satisfied religion of earlier times in order to draw people back to God. God sent these nagging spokesmen (and he still does) because he is committed to us. He wants desperately for us to recognize that. Only disloyal people give up or give in. But God does neither.

Radical Love

Jesus Christ verified the utter integrity of God's loyalty. In Jesus we learn that God's commitment is inextinguishable. God himself reached out to us. This was the broken father searching for a wayward son. This was an old woman frantically looking for a lost coin. This was the shepherd scouring the cliffs and ravines for a lost sheep (Lk 15).

This was God come as man. Jesus the Christ was humbled before us all; he received our blows, accepted our jeers, stooped to wash our feet. He was killed by us and he died for us. He climbed up on a cross to do what only God could do, die for an intractable people and repair the broken relationship between God and the people he created. This was also man rising from the dead to join the Father in heaven, where Jesus represents us as our worthy Advocate. By now we should get the point. Jesus Christ proves that God is radically loyal. Nothing can dissuade him from remaining so.

The apostle Paul pushed language to its limits and logic to its perfection when, in a series of questions, he pointed to Christ as proof of God's allegiance to us.

What then shall we say to this? If God is for us, who is against us? He who did not spare his own Son but gave him up for us all, will he not also give us all things with him? Who shall bring any charge against God's elect? It is God who justifies; who is to condemn? Is it Christ Jesus who died, yes, who was raised from the dead, who is at the right hand of God, who indeed intercedes for us? Who shall separate us from the love of Christ? Shall tribulation, or distress, or persecution, or famine,

or nakedness, or peril, or sword? (Rom 8:31-35)
Many of us might chafe at the very word *loyalty* because it evokes images of some insecure, demagogic leader demanding absolute, insufferable loyalty from his subordinates while he remains loyal only to himself. God's loyalty is all the more incredible because it originates in God's own character. He is the committed one. It is the superior who is loyal to the inferior. Our loyalty, however great, only mirrors his own.

Faith's Foundation
God's commitment to us is foundational for the Christian life because it makes his commitment, and not ours, the primary one. God is simply more committed to us than we are to him. His loyalty is like a mother's to her newborn baby. There is little that he expects from us, at least at first. That we exist is enough. That we have the capacity to know and love him makes him persist in loving us. His loyalty to us is what makes our commitment to him possible in the first place. God's loyalty to us not only precedes ours to him, but it also draws ours forth, as the warmth of spring stimulates the sprouting of all things green and lovely.

Further, the radical commitment of God toward us is foundational because it puts sin and guilt in its proper perspective. Not that we should treat sin more lightly, but we should view God as being greater than our sin. We usually do just the opposite. Too often we say to ourselves, "If God only knew what I was really like"—usually right after repeating a sin we have committed a hundred times before. We cannot believe that God is still loyal even after we have done such terrible deeds or caressed such ugly thoughts.

God, of course, is never as overwhelmed by our sin as we may be. He is not surprised by what he sees, however sordid or repetitious our deeds are. He knows us too well. He is bothered by our sin, yes. It breaks his heart. But he is more disturbed by our unwillingness to embrace the forgiveness he offers. He detests the kind of pride that makes us think we are too sinful for forgiveness, and he knows how presumptuous we are to think we could actually merit it by feeling bad about it long enough. That is indeed an insult to the work of Jesus Christ. Yet even such pride does not push God to disloyalty; it only blinds us to the great love God has for us.

God's loyalty is also foundational because it stops us from defining Christianity in terms of our personal performance and religious achievements. Many of us live as if the Christian life were a matter of feelings about God and duties done for God. We live as religious egotists. We say that we are doing well with God if *we* are disciplined or if *we* are obeying him. We think that we are close to God if *we* feel close to him. We believe that Christianity is true if *we* have been made happy and successful by it or if our religious techniques work. We delude ourselves by thinking, "If only I could conquer this nagging problem, then I would be a true Christian." For many of us, our Christian faith is as good as we are, not as good as God is.

But as long as we make our feelings, our discipline, our consistency, our techniques and our success and happiness the foundation for Christian living, we shall never know true Christianity. It always begins with God, never with us. He is loyal. That is the most basic truth. "If we are faithless, he remains faithful—for he cannot deny himself" (2 Tim 2:13; see also Rom 3:3-4).

Learning to Rest

Christians who understand this foundational principle find deep security and stability. Hudson Taylor, a famous nineteenth-century missionary to China, learned it late in his life. He had served in China for years, accomplishing what few others would hardly dream of. Yet he still thought he was a spiritual failure. He believed that a renewed commitment to discipline would relieve him, but such rigor only drove him to despair. In a letter to his sister he described his condition:

But personal need stood first and was the greatest. I felt the ingratitude, the danger, the sin of not living nearer to God. I prayed, agonized, fasted, strove, made resolutions, read the Word more diligently, sought more time for meditation—but all without avail. Every day, almost every hour, the consciousness of sin oppressed me. . . . I knew that if only I could abide in Christ all would be well, but I could not. I would begin the day with prayer, determined not to take my eye off Him for a moment, but pressure of duties, sometimes very trying, and constant interruptions apt to be so wearing, caused me to forget Him. . . . Each day brought its register of sin and failure, of lack of power. . . . Instead of growing stronger, I seemed to be getting weaker and to have less power against sin; and no wonder, for faith and even hope were getting low. I hated myself, I hated my sin, yet gained no strength against it. . . . I thought that holiness, practical holiness, was to be gradually attained by a diligent use of the means of grace. There was nothing I so much desired as holiness, nothing I so much needed; but far from any measure attaining it, the more I strove after it, the more it evaded my grasp; until hope itself almost died out.[2]

Taylor agonized over what he considered to be the worst of sins: unbelief. When his condition of torment and guilt was at its worst, he received a letter from a friend. One phrase in the letter liberated Taylor. He wrote to his sister about it later:

But how to get faith strengthened? Not by striving after faith, but by resting on the Faithful one: As I read, I saw it all! "If we believe not, he abideth faithful!" I looked to Jesus and saw (and when I saw, oh, how joy flowed!) that He has said, "I will never leave Thee!" "Ah, *there* is rest!" I thought. I have striven in vain to rest in Him. I'll strive no more. For has not *He* promised to abide with me—never to leave me, never to fail me?[3]

Taylor learned that God is committed to us. God's undying loyalty led to Christ's death. His unyielding faithfulness yielded to the hate and violence of humanity. His all-embracing steadfastness embraced even suffering. His loyalty frees us, in our weakness, cowardice and fear, to become ever more loyal to God.

Were the whole realm of nature mine,
That were a present far too small;
Love so amazing, so divine,
Demands my soul, my life, my all.[4]

Study Questions

1. Do you ever feel guilty, even after confessing sin? Do you feel like a failure as a disciple of Christ? Do your emotions fluctuate from religious ecstasy to spiritual depression? What causes these feelings?

2. How does the author describe God's loyalty? What do we learn about God's loyalty from Psalm 139:1-18? from Romans 8:28-39?

3. Why do you think it is so hard for Christians to believe that God is loyal to them?

4. What happens to believers when they do affirm God's loyalty? How does it affect the problems mentioned in question 1?

Chapter 4

A COMPELLING
CHARACTER

I SOON DISCOVERED that there was more to the Sage than an interesting past and an ability to tell a good story. I learned he was a man of insight. I saw this for the first time when I accompanied him to a grocery store in town. He needed to do some shopping and had invited me along. I was standing in one of the store aisles surveying the cereals when I heard, very faintly, a subdued conversation. The two boys obviously didn't know I could hear them.

"What're you doing?" one of them asked in a surprised voice.

"Putting some of this stuff in my pockets," the other whispered inpatiently.

"What if you get caught?"

"We won't."

"What do you mean 'we'? I'm not takin' nothin'."

"If I get caught, you'll get caught. We're in this together."

"Then put that stuff back!"

"Wait! Listen to me first, chicken face. You go up to the old man at the cash register and ask him a question or something."

"Like what?"

"I don't know. Like, 'Where's your bathroom?' or 'Do you sell candy here?' Something like that. Just make sure his back is turned to the door. While you do that, I'll sneak out with this stuff and a couple of bags of doughnuts."

"If we get caught I'll kill you."

"We won't. Just do what I told you. And don't choke."

Just then the Sage, pushing a cart heaped with groceries, rounded the corner. He spoke to me before I could get a word out.

"Store sure is empty today," he said. "These little places can't compete with the supermarket chains anymore. That's sad, really. No more personal touch. Say, did you find the cereals your mother wanted?"

"Listen," I said. "I just overheard a conversation between two kids. They're planning to steal some stuff. I think we should do something."

With me leading the way, we walked hurriedly to the end of the aisle. We spotted the owner just as one of the boys, rough looking and about fifteen years old, was turning away from him to walk out the door. Before we could say anything, the owner saw the other boy running across the parking lot. No doubt suspicion made him move toward the door. And when a bag of doughnuts dropped from the boy's coat, he realized he'd been tricked. The second boy dashed out the door, grabbed the bag of doughnuts and ran after the first. The owner pursued both of them, yelling and cursing at the top of his lungs.

A few minutes later he returned, tired and furious. By that time we were standing at the check-out.

"Little punks," he said in disgust. "I don't know why I let 'em in the store. Either they steal me blind or they give me food stamps."

"Happen to you often?" the Sage asked as he unloaded the cart.

"Often enough," the owner said. "I'd like to refuse them service, but I'd probably get in trouble with the law."

"Hard to run a store alone," said the Sage.

"Not if we didn't have migrants around. I wonder sometimes whether it's worth growin' fruit up here. Just attracts the sorta scum we don't want. Rats! I wish I could catch one of 'em. I'd teach him a lesson he'd never forget."

Back at the cabin the Sage and I talked about the incident.

"What did you think of the owner?" I asked. "I mean, how he reacted."

"Not a lot of compassion," he said.

"I don't blame him," I said in his defense.

"I don't fault him for his anger," he said.

"Then how can you say he lacked compassion?" I asked.

"Because I think a person can be angry and compassionate at the same time."

"How?"

"Because true character contains opposites. The people I've grown to respect always have opposites in them. You know—discipline and freedom, confidence and humility, even anger and compassion. That to me is what made Jesus so engaging. He had those same opposites, like kindness and severity."

"So you don't think the owner was wrong in being mad?" I said.

"No. I'd have been mad, too."

"And compassionate as well?"

"Perhaps not, but I'd like to think so."

*   *   *

Opposites Attract

Some people attract us, not because of their looks or what they do, but because of who they are. Something about them draws us to them. It compels us to investigate. It invites us to get to know them. It makes us *want* to know them better. What is it?

Character. Character attracts because it makes an ordinary person extraordinary. It takes a flat personality and adds new dimensions to it. Ultimately, character makes a person bigger than what we would naturally allow or expect. It makes a person hard to figure out or control.

A person with character has what appear to be contradictory qualities, as the Sage pointed out. Kindness and anger, for example, can describe a person who loves people but hates sin. Jesus is the ultimate model for character because he was forever breaking out of the boxes people put him in. Just when the Pharisees were ready to write him off for his spineless acceptance of sinners, he preached the demanding message of the Sermon on the Mount. Just when his acts of power were tempting his disciples to crown him a political king, he wrapped himself in a towel and washed their feet. Jesus reflected the character of God because, of course, he was God.

God's character is another source for discipleship. While God's commitment provides a stable foundation for our faith, God's character attracts us to him and compels us to know him. In fact, it is impossible *not* to want to know him once we grasp the essentials of his character.

Why? Because people who unite opposites within them and make them work together command our respect and gain our attention. For example, good parents are both tender and tough, and so inspire love and obedience. True heroes are both courageous and humble, and so compel us to follow their example. Good bosses are both demanding and unassuming, and so challenge us to do our best. People having such opposites cannot be so easily pigeonholed and dismissed. They arouse our interest. They earn our admiration. They surprise us with the appropriateness and creativity of every move they make, like a musician who seems to pick just the right music for the right occasion. Their character attracts us.

The Lion and the Lamb
God, too, appears to unite opposites. He is, for example, both *holy* and *loving*. He is like a gentle parent; we are to call him "Father" (Heb 12:5-6). But he is also likened to a consuming fire (Heb 12:29). We are commanded, therefore, to fear him as we seek him.

Likewise, God is both *sovereign* and *suffering*. He is transcendent and mighty, the Creator of the world. God alone is great, the ruler over all of history, the Alpha and the Omega. He is powerful, able to bring good out of the greatest evil. Yet God suffers for the very world he made, and he even came in Jesus Christ to die for it. Though infinitely exalted over creation, he subjected himself to creation's worst bondage, death.

Further, God is both *universal* and *particular*. He is universal in that he is eternal. He is not bound by time. Every moment in history is the present to God. The psalmist says:

Lord, thou hast been our dwelling place in all generations.

Before the mountains were brought forth,
　or ever thou hadst formed the earth and the world,
　from everlasting to everlasting thou art God. (Ps 90:1-2)

God is also universal in that he is omnipresent. He is not bound by space:

Whither shall I go from thy Spirit?
　Or whither shall I flee from thy presence?
If I ascend to heaven, thou art there!
　If I make my bed in Sheol, thou are there!
If I take the wings of the morning
　and dwell in the uttermost parts of the sea,
even there thy hand shall lead me,
　and thy right hand shall hold me. (Ps 139:7-10)

Yet God revealed himself to a particular man, Abraham, at a particular time in history and in a particular place. Later he formed a particular nation, Israel. Finally, he was incarnated as a particular person, Jesus Christ. The eternal God, the ever-present God, bound himself to the particulars of time and space.

God is both *unchanging* and *flexible*. We extol his unchanging character in hymns:

Great is thy Faithfulness, O God my Father,
There is no shadow of turning with Thee;
Thou changest not, Thy compassions they fail not;
As Thou has been Thou forever wilt be.[5]

Yet we learn in the Bible that God changes his mind, adapts to irregular circumstances and shows flexibility in adjusting to the capricious will of man (Ex 32:9-14).

Finally, God is both *omniscient* and *gracious*. He knows everything: past, present and future, all the mysteries of life, all goodness and beauty, the innermost secrets of man, the whole of truth. And his perfect knowledge is not morally neutral. He also knows everything in the sense that he defends goodness and judges evil, upholds truth and exposes falsehood. He *must* do this, for he is goodness; he is truth. His presence cannot tolerate corruption, deception and immorality. Yet he is also gracious. He forgives and forgets.

> The LORD is merciful and gracious,
>> slow to anger and abounding in steadfast love.
> He will not always chide,
>> nor will he keep his anger for ever.
> He does not deal with us according to our sins,
>> nor requite us according to our iniquities. (Ps 103:8-10)

Creative Tension

Such is the tension within the character of God. It compels us to closely investigate. It catches us by surprise. Just when we think we have him figured out and under our intellectual control, the light of his life shifts, causing his revelation and his character to take on a slightly different color. We know he is loving, but then we discover he is also holy. We know he suffered, and then we learn that he is also sovereign. He is always greater, his character more expansive and extreme, than we thought before. Yet he is simple; he is one. He has all these qualities at the same time, and they are somehow consistent within him.

Some of our greatest hymns capture this peculiar combination of qualities within the Godhead. Consider the first two stanzas of Walter Chalmers Smith's hymn:

> Immortal, invisible, God only wise,
> In light inaccessible hid from our eyes,
> Most blessed, most glorious, the Ancient of Days,

Almighty, victorious, thy great name we praise.
Unresting, unhasting, and silent as light,
Nor wanting, nor wasting, Thou rulest in might;
Thy justice like mountains high soaring above
Thy clouds, which are fountains of goodness and love.[6]

We dare not disregard this tension. If we do and concentrate on just a few of God's qualities to the neglect of others, we will compromise our knowledge of God and lose our longing for God. This has often happened in the past, and it happens still today. At times, intellectual attention to the "transcendent" qualities of God has overshadowed the equally important "condescendent" or personal qualities of God. Some of the early church fathers tried to accommodate theology to Greek philosophy. Words like "eternal," "immense," "infinite" and "immutable" were used, thus making theology too abstract and God too conceptual and distant. He could be contemplated and analyzed, but not loved and trusted.

Both the Protestant and Catholic wings of the church have, at times, drifted too far in the same direction. Consider this definition of God from Vatican I:

... mighty, eternal, immense, incomprehensible, infinite in his intellect and will and in all perfection. As He is one unique and spiritual substance, entirely simple and unchangeable, we must proclaim Him distant from the world in existence and essence, blissful in Himself and from Himself, ineffably exalted above all things that exist or can be conceived besides Him.[7]

There is nothing incorrect about this definition. Still, it tends to negate everything personal and familiar to us. Is this the only way to think about God?

We can also conceive of God in a very personal way. Sometimes our attitude toward God becomes too chummy. He is our best friend. We liken him to a good coach, a popular motivator, a positive thinker, the big Guy in the sky. We use earthly and trivial analogies to make him seem more real; but we disregard his unspeakable greatness. He is there when we need him; he is our entertainer, therapist, cheerleader. He is no longer the Lord.

A predominance of one or the other aspect of God's character leads to bi-theism. God the Father is one kind of being: sovereign, holy, unchanging, wrathful, omniscient, someone to fear when we sin and cry out to when we are in serious trouble. God the Son is another kind of being: kind, loving, approachable, understanding, one with whom we can share our problems. We divide God and Jesus in the same way traditional homes divide the roles and personalities of father and mother. It creates a schizophrenic religion.

The Bible—not abstract thought or popular thinking—must be the source of our knowledge about God. He is, as we have observed, both one thing and its opposite—holy *and* loving, for example. If he were merely loving, we would presume upon his goodness; if he were merely holy, we would flee from him. Love and holiness draw us into the heart of God.

Such is the character of God and the power of opposites within him. He is worthy of reverence; he is ripe for a relationship. If his loyalty provides us with security and stability in our faith, his character gives us motivation and desire to understand him and know him better. Incredibly, as that happens, we will take on the same character he has. "Beloved, we are God's children now; it does not yet appear what we shall be, but we know that when he appears we shall be *like him*, for we shall see him as he is" (1 Jn 3:2).

Study Questions
1. Describe someone you know who has "strong character."
2. Why do people with "strength of character" tend to stand out? Why are there so few people like that?
3. As you review the life of Christ as presented in the Gospels, how would you describe Jesus' character? (For every attribute mentioned in the chapter, think of a specific instance in Jesus' life that evidences this attribute.)
4. The God we know determines the kind of religion we have and the kind of persons we become. How do you think people undermine the biblical view of God? How does this affect their religion? their character?
5. Are there any ways in which your view of God is distorted? What attributes of God do you need to appreciate more? How can you do this?

Chapter 5

THE PLEASURE
OF INTIMACY

ABOUT A WEEK AFTER OUR visit to the grocery store the Sage had his first dinner at my house. After the meal my mom and dad dutifully cleared the dishes, a task from which I had been released that night for some "special reason," as my mother said.

When they returned from the kitchen, my mom was triumphantly carrying a German chocolate cake. With a glimmer in her eye and a puckish grin on her face, she set it down right in front of me and said, "Surprise!"

"Mom, you shouldn't have," I said. "When did you find the time?"

"I didn't," she said.

"Dad, did you bake this cake? I didn't know you had it in you."

"I didn't, and I don't," he said, smiling like a Cheshire cat.

I looked at my sister, but she only shook her head, disclaiming all responsibility. Then I spied the Sage out of the corner of my eye. "Did you bake this for me? How did *you* know it was my favorite?"

"Don't look at me," he said. "That's not my handiwork."

"Then who baked it?" I asked impatiently. I knew that they were up to something.

"There's a card with it," my mother said, this time finding it impossible to restrain a big smile. "Why don't you open it up and read it to us?"

"I will!" my sister said as she snatched the card.

"No you won't," I snapped, grabbing the card from her. I noticed immediately that it smelled sweet and perfumy. I studied the handwriting; it was too neat to give any clues. Then, before opening it, I peeked at my family and the Sage, who were looking like a pack of hyenas peering at a helpless victim.

"All right," I said. "What's the big deal? Don't you know it's impolite to stare? It's not *my* fault I got this cake!"

"Just interested, that's all," my dad said. Then he turned to the Sage and said, as if speaking to him privately, "You know, William, our son has quite a problem with women. They keep chasing him. Why, when we're at home, this happens three or four times a week!"

"Come off it, Dad!" I said. "That's a big lie and you know it."

"Open the card," my sister screamed. "I can't wait to see who it's from."

So I did. I scanned it to see whether or not it was safe enough to read aloud. It wasn't. But I decided to read it anyway, since I knew they would seize it by force if I didn't. The poetry was bad but effective:

This cake, from one who admires
　But whose personality retires—
　　from you whom she aspires
　　　to know.

Taste all that's sweet,

This for you a treat,
Until this fall we meet—
at some arranged hour.

You will know the cake's cook
When I enter your little black book
By asking you to look—
for me—on the third day of school.

Then you will know, so be wary.
Until that time—
eat, drink and be merry.

Love. . . ?

P.S. See you at college.

My family gave her a standing ovation, while I asked, all too predictably, "I wonder who it could be?"

And I did wonder, especially after eating a piece of the cake, which
rivaled my mother's most brilliant efforts. The whole experience
was wonderful, being only slightly marred by the battering I received from my family, who could hardly eat their dessert because
they were teasing me so much. Even the Sage was rascally. He
couldn't, or wouldn't, stop laughing whenever he looked at me.

After dessert we retired to the living room. The laughter had
subsided by then, but not my curiosity. I kept reviewing the names
of the girls in my class who would be likely candidates for coming
up with such an outrageous idea.

"You know," the Sage said after a few moments of silence, "that
cake and note just made me recall a childhood memory. I can't
believe it. I had completely forgotten about it."

"What is it?" my dad asked.

"I was twelve or thirteen at the time. We lived in Brooklyn. One
day—it was in the middle of the summer, if I remember correctly—

I found a baseball on the front porch of my house. A note was attached to it. It said that a boy my age should have his own baseball and that this one was a gift from someone who wanted to make me happy. That was it. Nothing else, not even a signature. I was simply delighted, for I loved baseball. Since my family wasn't very rich, we didn't get gifts like that very often.

"Naturally I wanted to find out who it was from. I investigated the clues I had, asked a few people in the neighborhood, but finally gave up. Soon I forgot about it.

"About a month later I found a baseball bat on the front porch. Again, an unsigned note was attached to it. This time I was more intent than ever on finding out who gave the bat. But I discovered nothing.

"For the next two years I received about eight or ten gifts: a baseball glove, baseball shoes, a mirror for my bicycle. Things like that. Every gift came with an unsigned note. I was utterly mystified."

"So what happened?" my dad asked.

"I wanted to know who that person was, and I guess I wanted to know that person *as a person*. The giver became more important than the gifts. Do you know what I mean? Whoever it was, I thought, must be a true friend."

"Did you ever find out?" my mom asked.

"Never. We lived in a crowded, close community. It could have been any one of two dozen people. I couldn't narrow it down. Whoever it was knew how to give gifts secretively."

"Well, I hope it won't be that hard to discover who baked the cake," I said.

"You'll find her," my dad said.

"But will I *like* her?"

"You'll find out," added Mom.

*　　　　　*　　　　　*

God's Pleasure
"You are my beloved son. With you I am very pleased." Such were

the words Jesus heard after his baptism. His high calling and noble character were being affirmed. The Father was taking pleasure in his Son.

God takes pleasure in us, too. "Work out your own salvation with fear and trembling," wrote Paul, "for God is at work in you, both to will and to work for his good pleasure" (Phil 2:12-13). God pronounced a "very good" after he had made us. We are deemed even better after he redeems us.

God is pleased with us when we know him as our God and acknowledge him as the center of life. He delights in us when we enjoy not just the gifts he gives, which are many, but the person he is. God's pleasure is thus another source for our discipleship because it reveals God's heart to us. While his loyalty makes us secure in a relationship with him and his character beckons us to know him, his pleasure reveals his desire to know us. It provides the impetus for intimacy with him. God is not merely tolerant of us. He loves us. He delights in us. He embraces us. Behind the bounty of gifts he gives is an affectionate heart, wooing us to him.

The Sage once said that the giver is better than the gift. However worthy of honor Edison's inventions are, *he* is worthy of the greater honor because they originated in his mind. Likewise, though I would relish the opportunity to stare at the ceiling of the Sistine Chapel, I would find equal enjoyment in knowing Michelangelo, for those magnificent paintings came from his hand. People err when they say that Christ's excellence consists in his miracles or teachings, for Christ's person holds supremacy over his work and words. The highest value in life is not to possess something but to know someone. People, not their deeds, are at the apex. God, not his gifts, is absolute. Knowing the Creator is better than enjoying the creation.

There is a double pleasure here. God takes pleasure in us, and we find our greatest pleasure in him. Ultimately his desires and our desires are one. As he yearns for us, so we yearn for him. Discipleship unites our longing hearts with his. Our knowledge of him is his delight and our satisfaction. There is absolute joy in knowing

God just as he feels joy in knowing us.

> The LORD is my chosen portion and my cup;
> > thou holdest my lot.
> The lines have fallen for me in pleasant places;
> > yea, I have a goodly heritage. . . .
> Thou dost show me the path of life;
> > in thy presence there is fulness of joy,
> > in thy right hand are pleasures for evermore. (Ps 16:5-6, 11)

The Pain of Fragmentation

Intimacy with God protects us from becoming fragmented by the competing interests of modern culture. Such fragmentation divides the soul. Instead of having one center around which life revolves, we have many, all vying for control. Once we stop seeking God, we ourselves become the sought—or better, the hunted. Desires, habits and idols begin to dominate our lives. We find ourselves being driven first by this habit and then by that interest, until we feel like we are being broken into a million pieces.

Fragmentation makes us unstable, fickle, double-minded. At one moment we want purity; the next we lust. Under certain conditions we feel confident; under others we feel inferior. Sometimes we are creative and kind; at other times we are lazy and churlish. "O God, I feel like my soul is a war zone!" we say to ourselves. Why do we have such violent swings of mood, desire, character? Because we lack a divine center, an ultimate reference point, true intimacy with the living God. Deprived of a relationship with a good God, we are dominated by many bad ones, all pretenders to the thrones of our lives.

As if the conflict within us were not bad enough already, it is made worse by the culture we live in. Modern culture defines life as ownership, consumption, competition. Just when we are beginning to feel comfortable having a certain personality, looking a certain way, associating with a certain group of friends and pursuing certain interests, along comes some new product, a new fad, a new idea or a new friend, and we are thrown once again into vertigo. Advertisements are particularly adept at making us feel that who we are and what we own is not good enough, that we simply *must* wash away the gray or buy a new car or drink a different beer. To find real happiness, we need more, always more. Life has become like one gigantic discount store; we have become mad shoppers.

Fragmentation makes us frenzied, superficial and careless. Instead of living life from the inside out, we live it from the outside in. We get busy, cramming more and more activities into our schedules without any purpose behind them. We get greedy, buying more and more products without any vision of stewardship. We race from one committee to the next, from one relationship to the next. We try to buy life as if it were a quantity of something we could find in a catalog. We become all motion, though we lack any direction. Thomas Merton writes:

> How many there are who are in a worse state still: They never even get as far as contemplation because they are attached to activities and enterprises that seem to be important. Blinded by their desire for ceaseless motion, for a constant sense of achievement, famished with a crude hunger for results, for visible and tangible success, they work themselves into a state in which they cannot believe that they are pleasing God unless they are busy with a dozen jobs at the same time.[8]

Only intimacy with God can deliver us from the problem of fragmentation. Surprisingly, God takes the initiative to develop such intimacy because he wants us to know him even when we lack the desire. He takes pleasure in the relationship he has with us, and he has created us with the same desire for intimacy. We will never be truly satisfied, then, however much we take advantage of the frills and fads of modern culture, until we cultivate a personal relationship with him.

The Spirit, Not the Senses

Intimacy with God, however, is not easy to develop. While we have the capacity for it, we have neglected that capacity by relying almost exclusively on our senses as the only way to gain sure knowledge of anything. Science and reason, good in themselves, have become so dominant in Western society that we have disregarded the other ways to perceive and know.

Our senses are not bad, but they are limited and can mislead us. We reduce life when we limit knowledge to that acquired by the senses alone. Can love be comprehended by them? Can wisdom be gained by them? God wants to enlarge our capacity to understand life and to perceive what is at the heart of it. He does not contradict the information we get from our senses, but he does transcend it. God purposes to give us knowledge of him first of all in our *spirits,* wherein lies the greatest potential for knowing him.

Our senses could not tolerate being exposed to God. A pure vision of him would overwhelm us and consume our senses. As the bright sun blinds the eye or a loud noise deafens the ear, so the greatness of God would obliterate our physical capacities. For a perfect, sensory knowledge of him we must wait until the resurrection, when we are given new bodies capable of being in the presence of God. In the meantime, we must look elsewhere. Carlo Carretto points to the darkness of faith as the answer. He believes that growth in the knowledge of God should be gradual, nurtured by faith, and not sudden, gained by sight.

The darkness is necessary, the darkness of faith is necessary, for God's light is too great. It wounds. I understand more and more that faith is not a mysterious and cruel trick of a God who hides himself without telling me why, but a necessary veil. My discovery of him takes place gradually, respecting the growth of divine life in me.[9]

While our senses limit us, at least in developing a relationship with God, our spirits do not. We have been given an inward capacity to know God, as if we have a sixth sense. It is possible to know God, then, and to know him well, without ever seeing, hearing or touching him. He imparts knowledge of himself to us in our spirits, provided we are open to him and eager to nurture this spiritual capacity for intimacy.

How can we cultivate this openness and discover this capacity?

Through solitude, worship and the sacraments.

Solitude

Solitude creates a space for God; it gives him room to work. Solitude also nurtures the divine center in us which was established when Christ entered our lives. Paul calls it, "Christ in you, the hope of glory." This divine center is the place where we can perceive that ultimate reality is determined by God alone. It is the place of true quiet and rest because it is the place in us where God lives and rules. It is the throneroom of God set up in the secret chamber of our hearts.

Suppose you are a king or queen, and your castle is being beseiged. So intense is the conflict that you can hardly think anymore. Your mind is cluttered with too many thoughts, your clothes sweaty and bloody, your body exhausted. Suddenly you remember something you had long forgotten. There is a small room in the center of the castle unknown to everyone except you. In that room is quiet and safety. There's a crystal ball there that will give you knowledge of the future. So you withdraw from the fighting for a few moments. You flee to your secret chamber and find rest. You gaze into the crystal ball and learn that your armies will win the battle. You are renewed and return to the combat with hope.

Solitude is a form of withdrawal; but it is not an escape. It is a way of building on Jesus Christ, the most solid foundation, the one who lives within us. Solitude requires a movement inward, not outward; we are able now to live from the inside out, not the outside in. Christ within us is the starting point of solitude.

David practiced solitude and with good reason. Life's circumstances were often unkind to him. He was hounded by King Saul, betrayed by the very people he had saved and deprived of his kingship. He learned how to move inwardly. He found stability in the secret places of his heart.

I lie in the midst of lions
that greedily devour the sons of men;
Their teeth are spears and arrows,

Their tongues sharp swords.
My heart is steadfast, O God,
   my heart is steadfast!
I will sing and make melody!
   Awake, my soul!
Awake, O harp and lyre!
   I will awake the dawn!
I will give thanks to thee, O Lord,
   among the peoples;
I will sing praises to thee among
   the nations.
For thy steadfast love is great to the heavens,
   thy faithfulness to the clouds. (Ps 57:4, 7-10)

Though solitude is a matter of the heart, we can encourage its development by learning to be physically alone with God. There the seeds of solitude are sown in receptive soil and protected from the inhospitable climate of the world. We must also learn to be *silent:* to listen, not talk; to wait, not act; to receive, not acquire. Enough of striving and racing! God invites us, the weary and heavy-laden, to find our rest in him. At first solitude will be obstructed by *our* thoughts, *our* concerns, *our* voices, *our* anxieties, by the need to write a letter to a friend or shop for groceries or write a paper. But in time we shall find ourselves plunging through the clutter of our world and into the reality of God's world. Noise will give way to silence; physical isolation to spiritual calm. Solitude will affect our being and spill over into everyday life. It will engender, as Nouwen says, the solitude of the heart.

But the solitude that really counts is the solitude of heart; it is an inner quality or attitude that does not depend on physical isolation. On occasion this isolation is necessary to develop this solitude of heart, but it would be sad if we considered this essential aspect of the spiritual life as a privilege of monks and hermits. It seems more important than ever to stress that solitude is one of the human capacities that can exist, be maintained and developed in the center of a big city, in the middle of a large crowd

and in the context of a very active and productive life.[10]
Solitude is not contemplation of the self but contemplation of God.
It does not engender laziness but gives us a quiet joy as we execute
all our responsibilities faithfully, both the important and mundane.
It does not nullify the need for community but enables us to see
other people from a divine perspective. It is not a spiritual emotion
but a movement to spiritual depth. Solitude pushes us to intimacy
with God. It gives God a space in our lives and gives our spirit a
chance to receive what God wants to impart—intimacy with himself. If we are willing to be silent before God and to dwell in that
inner chamber, we will discover that solitude can nurture a spirit
of calm in our lives. "Be still, and know that I am God" (Ps 46:10).

Worship

The word *worship* denotes ascribing supreme worth to something
and is used of our attitudes and actions toward whatever we su-
premely value in life. Since God by definition is at the center of life,
we can ultimately worship only him. To worship God rightly, we
must be willing to acknowledge him as God, give thanks to him and
surrender to him as the Lord of the universe. The two Old Testament words for worship are also sometimes translated from the
Hebrew as "to prostrate oneself" and "to serve." This indicates that
God is best worshiped either by falling on our faces before him or
by obeying his commands. Both are reasonable ways of ascribing
worth to him.

There are three essential elements to worship. *Form* enables us to
worship God, given our creatureliness. We must use language, ritual and liturgy. God even ordained this to be so. The Old Testament
form of worship made use of psalms, choirs, instruments and
prayers. The early church used hymns, prayers, the sacraments and
the gifts of the Spirit. Paul enjoined the church in Corinth to do all
things decently and in order, "for God is not a God of confusion but
of peace" (1 Cor 14:33).

Since form, however, can tend to become hollow, we are also
commanded to worship with our *hearts*. Our internal disposition

must be persuaded by the work of the Holy Spirit to delight in God. The eyes of our hearts must be enlightened. We must ask God to transform our affections.

Still, mere heartfelt worship is incomplete unless we use our *minds*. Our God is a God of truth. Our feelings about God are important, but they become useless unless we also have knowledge about God. We must learn to think about God. We must concentrate on the words of the hymns and litanies; we must weigh the words of the preacher; we must actively pray with the worship leader. Our minds must be engaged.

These three elements ought to be used as we praise God, which is the highest expression of worship. Praise enables us to consider the character of God and to adore his excellence. It helps us to concentrate on who God is, as he revealed himself in nature, in history and in Jesus Christ. Praise thus establishes an environment in which the reality of God is made supreme. It is like turning the thermostat to seventy degrees Fahrenheit. Life with God thrives under those conditions. In the midst of the incredible pessimism of Psalm 22, for example, David surprises us with these words: "Yet thou art holy, enthroned on the praises of Israel" (v. 3). By praising God, David was able to see the reign of God penetrate even the darkness of his suffering. Praise altered the atmosphere of his life. It can do the same for us. Thus, in addition to practicing solitude as a way of gaining intimate knowledge of God, we should also learn to worship God, especially in praise. This should be done daily and verbally, in obedience to the Scriptures: "Through [Christ] then let us continually offer up a sacrifice of praise to God, that is, the fruit of lips that acknowledge his name" (Heb 13:15).

The Sacraments
A third way we can nurture intimacy with God is by participating in the sacraments of communion and baptism. These constitute part of the ritual of the church. To some the sacraments might appear to be so ordinary, too simple, and therefore meaningless. Why then are they considered to be so powerful?

The rule of God over all of life, both material and immaterial, cannot be directly perceived by our senses. For us to cross the boundary between material and spiritual reality, therefore, we must have a medium—something earthly that points beyond itself to something otherworldly. These mediums we call "rituals," the sacraments being two of the rituals of the church. These are like windows that enable us to gaze into another world and experience its power. They point to a truth that is higher, richer and fuller than the tangible materials which are the mediums of the sacraments themselves: bread, wine and water.

Thus baptism points to the purity of heaven. Communion helps us to behold the power of forgiveness, the depth of God's sacrificial love and the wonder of the future feast we will enjoy in the age to come. But more, the sacraments flow two ways. Not only are we allowed to *see* spiritual reality, as if we were the spectators of heaven's events, but we are also invited to *receive* the substance of this reality in our lives. In the sacraments God imparts to us forgiveness, renewal, wisdom, power and life. In a sense, baptism and the Lord's Supper are doors that connect two worlds. We cross over from our world, the world of shadow, the earthly womb, to the world of substance and eternity. And we learn that our world only dimly reflects something much greater—spiritual reality.

The elements themselves are significant. The water of baptism cleanses and refreshes us. The bread and wine of the Eucharist nourish and sustain us. These elements are like food staples, the kinds of things we would want after a long trek through the desert.

And rightly so, for life *is* like a desert for true pilgrims. Yes, there are moments of plenty and grandeur when we feast on the fat of the land and journey through plush meadows and forestlands. But these moments are rare. Most of the time life is more stark and stripped, desertlike. What we long for is water to wash us, bread to feed us, wine to quench us. Communion is the Christian's food; baptism, our bath. They have meaning only to the dirty, hungry, thirsty traveler.

Finally, the sacraments enable us to participate in something greater than ourselves. They are the means by which to identify with the benevolent kingship of God. As a whole school participates vicariously in the successes of its basketball team by wearing buttons and going to the games or as thousands of teen-agers participate in the mystical power of popular culture by attending rock concerts, so we can participate in the victory of Christ's life, death and resurrection through baptism and communion. Christ's death becomes ours; his triumph our triumph. The sacraments are the rituals that remind us of whom we belong to. They are marks of our true identity. By them we affirm that we are children of God.

The Sage lamented his failure to find the mysterious person who had given him so many valuable gifts. Fortunately, we do not face the same frustration. We are privileged to know the Giver of every perfect gift. He is better than his gifts, for he is their Creator, the source of their life. Indeed, he is life itself. He is worthy to know.

Incredibly, God's pleasure is that we know him. We find our greatest pleasure in that, too. Even God's loyalty is a meaningless concept unless we see it as an invitation to plunge into an intimate relationship with God. What draws us to know God, then, is God's desire for us. God's pleasure is the source of our life in God. God wants a relationship with us. That helps us to discover what we want, and need—a relationship with him. "For with thee is the fountain of life; in thy light do we see light" (Ps 36:9).

Study Questions
1. God wants to know us. He takes pleasure in us. That is particularly significant today considering the rootless, fragmented society in which we live. What are some of the signs of our culture's fragmentation?
2. How has this affected our identities? goals? relationships? values?
3. Read Psalms 145—150. What is praise? How can we make praise a functional part of our lives?
4. Read Psalms 63 and 57. What is solitude? How can we practice it?
5. Read Matthew 28:18-20 and 1 Corinthians 11:17-34. What sacraments are mentioned here? How can we make them a more meaningful part of the life of the church?
6. What do you think you need to do to nurture intimacy with God?

III
GOD'S GOAL
FOR OUR
GROWTH

The source of discipleship is God—his loyalty, character and pleasure. He gives us the security and freedom to know him and grow in him. But discipleship also has a direction. Christians are part of a history that began with Abraham and will end when Christ returns to create new heavens and a new earth. This history, which we will explore in chapter six, tells the story of how God plans to use us to reclaim the earth which, by virtue of creation, rightfully belongs to him. To accomplish this plan God wills to make us into *new persons* (chapter seven); he purposes to establish a *new community* (chapter eight); and he plans to create a whole *new world* (chapter nine). He will do all of this through Jesus Christ (chapter ten). We begin, then, with another sketch from my summer with the Sage. By recounting an unforgettable relationship he had with a janitor, the Sage showed me something important about a biblical view of history.

Chapter 6

HISTORY'S
DRAMA

WHEN I WASN'T WORKING, lunch was my favorite time of day. I often joined the Sage at his cabin. We always sat on the front porch, rain or shine, to relish Michigan's summer fruit and read the morning paper. Though we began our ritual in silence, it rarely ended up that way. Some article on the front page or in the editorial section would prompt one of us to make a comment, and soon we would begin an intense debate. I learned to deftly defend and argue my opinions. The Sage had exacting standards for conversation. He believed that people should think before they speak, especially when discussing his two favorite topics, politics and religion.

One particular afternoon I was reading an article about Nixon's upcoming visit to Europe, which was deemed by the press to be a politically astute act. After finishing the article, I put the paper on my lap, reached for a few grapes and sighed.

"What's on your mind?" the Sage asked.

"I'm wondering what it would be like to be famous."

"What do you mean by *famous?*"

"You know, to be in a position where we could make history, where we could do something important and memorable."

"So you don't think that you and I will ever have much impact on history?"

"Not really," I said. "We're the people that history happens to."

"I'm not sure I agree," he said. "It depends on what you mean by history. I think most of us conceive of history in a way that keeps us out of its making: we're the ones history shapes; we're not history shapers."

"What's wrong with that?" I asked. "Do you think everybody can be famous?"

"There's a great deal wrong with it," he said. "For one thing, it makes us passive and indifferent, the mere victims of events happening to us. For another, it makes us selfish. If the course of history can't be altered by us, for good or evil, then why not live for ourselves? Most importantly, your view of history excludes common people. Have they no significance?"

"Of course they do! All people are important to God."

"But are they important *for history?* I think that they are. Let me explain why. About ten years ago I got to know the janitor of my office building in New York. He was a lively fellow, always witty and friendly. He loved to read, and his favorite topics of conversation were . . ."

". . . politics and religion," I interrupted.

"How did you guess?" the Sage replied. "Anyway, I always wondered why he was a janitor. It seemed to me that he was too energetic and intelligent for that kind of job. One day I asked him, and he told me his life story. He was married at a young age, eighteen, I think. He and his wife had planned to work a few years before they both went on to school—she to be a musician, he to be a lawyer. He insisted, however, that she attend college first, a very unusual decision in that day. A man's career always took precedence over a woman's. They saved up enough money for her to enroll at Columbia University, where she earned her degree. Meanwhile, he worked two jobs, as a janitor and as a cook on weekends.

"Then she got pregnant. Again and again. They had four children in six years. Naturally he couldn't leave his jobs, at least not until all the children were in school. Several years later, however, his wife became ill with cancer. After fighting it for three years, she died. To care for the children, he hired a housekeeper and kept his two jobs. He never left them."

"What happened to the kids?" I asked.

"It's incredible," the Sage said. "Every one of them went on to excel in their professions. Two of them are doctors. The third won a seat in the state house where he is still serving. The youngest is a fine musician. I heard her sing with the Grand Rapids Symphony earlier this summer, right after I arrived from New York.

"What's more, they all adore their father. They have begged him to quit his job, but he refuses. He says that there are too many people who need his help. And I agree. He's the de facto minister and therapist at my old office building."

"So he's making history," I said. "Is that what you learned?"

"Yes, that's what I learned," he said. "His example was one of the reasons why I eventually left the law firm and joined the public defender's office in New York City. I didn't want to be famous anymore. I wanted to be faithful."

"Did you ever go back?"

"Never," the Sage said.

*   *

Playing Our Parts

Few people have a sense of destiny. Few people believe that they are part of a movement that will lead to a wonderful ending. Few people, therefore, live for something that is greater than themselves. Why should they?

Christians believe, however, that God is the Lord of history. Discipleship requires that we begin to see ourselves as participants in his history and as shapers of a history he ultimately controls. God has written a historical drama; he has chosen his cast; now he is pressing us (for *we* are the principal players in the drama) to play our parts well. Of course we do not know all the details yet. Some of the props are unfamiliar. A few of the characters are still strangers to us. The plot, too, has taken surprising turns, both wonderful and tragic. Yet we know that the drama has been written, staged and is being directed by God himself. That is all the security we need.

There is a direction to discipleship. God has a goal in mind. He created this world to be the habitation of creatures who were made in his image. But we rebelled and were conquered by evil. God plans now to reclaim and restore what is rightfully his. And he purposes to do it through us. History is the story of how he began to reclaim the world, how he continues his work and how he plans to finish it.

Act One

The first scene of this drama tells the story of one man, Abraham. God summoned Abraham from his home in Ur and from his polytheism to follow a new God, the one true God, to a new land (Gen 12—25). God promised to make of Abraham a great name (Gen 12:1-3), reversing the ambition of the builders of Babel, who wanted to "make a name" for themselves (Gen 11). Abraham was called to be God's man, the recipient of God's favor, the fruit of God's discipline, the symbol of the prosperity and fullness God intends for all people. God gave Abraham *status* by calling him into a relationship with himself. But he also built *stature* in him, so that Abraham began to be the kind of person God intends all people to be. Through him God also established a new heritage. God became known as the God of Abraham, Isaac and Jacob (Ex 3:6). Abraham is therefore a model of the *new person* God wants to create through his drama.

A few more lines, a change of scene, an unusual twist of plot and the drama races on to the character of Joseph (Gen 37—50). His brothers betrayed him and sent him to Egypt, where he became a slave and later a prisoner. Yet in time—God's time as it turns out—he became second in command over the greatest power on earth, the Egyptian Empire. Joseph's story establishes the connection between popular history and biblical history, how the one becomes the setting in which real history, God's history, unfolds. Through Joseph's leadership the drama was propelled forward. The people of God settled in Egypt, where they found a place of quiet and plenty.

Four hundred years later Moses appeared. Though born an Israelite and condemned to die in infancy, he was rescued by a maid of Pharaoh's daughter and brought up an Egyptian. As an adult he could have enjoyed the wealth and splendor of the palace, but he chose instead to identify with his own people, who were new slaves in Egypt. Later he faced Pharaoh—this time as an adversary, not as a son—and proved once again that real history is made by the few who challenge the values of secular history by daring to believe in God. The people of Israel were delivered from bondage and led to the Promised Land. Through Moses' leadership God established a *new community*. God gave them a new set of standards by which to live. He protected them with supernatural power. He charged them to be faithful to him.

Others joined the cast. Joshua was a man of war. His expedition into Palestine showed that God's people were destined to conquer. As long as the people lived obediently, God promised to fight for them. The battles under Joshua also forewarned the people of Israel that their high status would bring both conflict and victory and that the clash between good and evil would be brutal. Joshua's leadership led Israel to a homeland. The long process of building a new world had thus begun.

The story of Rahab shows how *inclusive* God's people were supposed to be. Rahab was a Gentile and a whore. But because she assisted two Israelites who came to spy on Jericho, she was delivered from destruction and found a place in the lineage of Jesus.

The book of Judges warns us of what happens when God's people compromise. God disciplined them for "doing what was right in their own eyes" but wrong in his. The judges—Gideon, Samson, Deborah and others—turned the tide of evil in the land only after the people were willing to repent.

The period of the monarchy (1 Samuel through 2 Kings) proved that Israel could be similar to and yet different from the nations surrounding her. By then she had the same institutions as the other nations (king, courts, armies), but built on different principles (justice and righteousness). David, the greatest of the kings, had a passion for God that drove him to explore music, dance, the art of kingship and worship. He showed how comprehensive God's *cultural penetration* should be.

The drama then turned tragic. After Solomon's death the nation split (1 Kings 12). Rehoboam assumed David's throne over the southern half of the kingdom, called Judah; Jeroboam ruled the northern kingdom, called Israel. The division was never healed, despite the warnings and pleadings of the prophets who called both nations to justice and peace. The prophets reminded the people that they were meant to build a different kind of community, one of love and loyalty, not one of blood and ease; and they told them that they were called to be a light to the world. But the people chose to remain deaf and blind. They did not want to be God's people on God's terms.

Still, God sent unlikely actors in those days: Jeremiah, the weeping prophet; Hosea, the husband of a whore; Isaiah, a man of noble blood; Amos, a farmer from the rural south. After the fall of Judah, which had outlived Israel by a hundred fifty years, God pushed Esther onto the center stage of history. She was a beautiful woman whose charm and wits preserved the people of God from annihilation. At the same time Nehemiah played the role of a great leader; Ezra, a radical reformer. To continue his plan, God began to work with a faithful remnant. Many of these figures, though famous now, were unknown in their day. We find no mention of them in secular history books. Back then God excelled in the unpredictable: strange turns of plot, unusual characters, unexpected appearances, peculiar changes of scene. He still does.

The Lead Character

Together all of these actors set the stage for the one entrance that mattered most. Jesus Christ plays the lead role in the drama of history. He was the promised seed of Adam, Abraham, Moses and David, destined to be a blessing to the whole world. He was the only remnant that remained.

He was a surprising figure. From a human point of view, he was average in every way. He dressed in a simple tunic, grew up as a common, uneducated man and attracted common, uneducated followers. He preached a message of the kingdom, though he had no throne, no army and no fortress. He possessed only a blameless character and incredible spiritual power. And he talked in the most unsettling way about grace, judgment, life and death. He lived out a set of principles that clarified in stark, demanding terms the intent of the Ten Commandments. He even claimed to be God.

He proved it, too. However insidiously the leaders undermined his message and opposed his ministry, he still conquered. Not even death could defeat him. Three days after his death he rose from the dead and rejoined his disciples, whom he charged and empowered to invade the world with the good news. Then he ascended into heaven. Jesus, then, was the fulfillment of all that went before. He was the ultimate example of the *new person;* he established a *new community;* he summoned his followers to build a *new world.*

Jesus entered human history to drive the drama to its spectacular climax. He will return before the final curtain falls. In the meantime, he has called us, his followers, to join the cast on stage, to take up the parts yet to be played so that we, like the first disciples, can help reclaim the lost world. The movement of God's history runs through the present, of which we are a part, and into the future, which we will help shape for good or evil.

The Supporting Cast

Such is the drama of history. We can learn at least three lessons from it. First, we observe that God uses common people (Rahab, Hannah, David, Peter) to make history. The powerful of society often form a background in which the little people, the faithful people, honor God and transform the world. God loves to use the unassuming, unimportant people in the world. He only requires us to say with Mary, "Let it be to me according to your word" (Lk 1:38).

There is no room for selfish ambition. Self-aggrandizement leads only to self-destruction. God looks for other qualities, like faithfulness in little tasks, love for all people, a prayerful posture in the face of biblical responsibilities. If we are students, we should be patient and diligent in our studies. If we are homemakers or executives, we should be joyful in our service. If we are professional athletes or entertainers, we should be modest and morally upright. Whatever we do, wherever we are, we should be content, believing that God will use our efforts to make history.

Second, this drama of history teaches us that Christianity is essentially a story. It is *the* story, toward which all other stories about gods, kings, knights, dragons and heroes point. The story of the Christian faith tells us that God, who was outside the material world and beyond space and time, entered this world as a person so that through his life and death we might become his people. God became a man that man might become like God. Such a story proves that the journeys of Odysseus, the quests of King Arthur and the good deeds of talking animals have a truth to them far more profound than we could ever have imagined. Our fantastic dreams of adventure have become a reality. The myth has become a fact. A far-fetched story has become history. Incredibly, we have been summoned to follow the hero into his eternal kingdom.

Third, we learn that history has two lines running through it. The first line is what we could call "popular history," the history of the famous, the powerful and the wealthy. The other is what we could call "biblical history," the history of the character and deeds of God's people. In the light of eternity the only line that matters is biblical history. Often these two lines run askew, going in different directions. At such times there appear to be no real connection between them, except the events of popular history create the setting for the movement of biblical history. Caesar Augustus ordered that a census be taken when Mary was pregnant. This forced Mary and Joseph to travel to Bethlehem where she gave birth to Jesus. While Augustus was admiring his domain, the Savior of the world was born in a hamlet on the far reaches of his empire. It was hardly an important event then. But it is now.

At other times these lines intersect. The two lines meet on the plane of history just long enough for opposing figures to glance at each other before continuing in their different directions. Moses met Pharaoh this way—one heading toward the Promised Land and the other toward defeat and death. Jesus stood only briefly before Pilate. Paul testified to Agrippa, Festus, Felix and perhaps even to the emperor Claudius. Chance meetings. Their paths intersected, but only for a time.

Occasionally these lines merge. The history of God's people and the history of popular culture join when God has an important task to accomplish or a message to give. God calls a society to repentance (Jonah), or some task for Christ's followers is so great that it requires the resources of the larger society (Acts), or an issue is so critical that the entire society must hear it (Isaiah). Joseph's exaltation in Egypt represents such a merging. Esther's benevolent intervention for the Jews in exile is another.

How should we then view history? Suppose that you are reading a novel about an aristocratic family. Even though many pages are devoted to the wealth, power and tragedies of the family and their friends, the main character of the book is an insignificant figure, the family butler, whose kindness, courage and wisdom save the family and eventually win the day. You realize this because you know how the novel ends. But within the novel itself another character appears, a writer and historian, who joins the family to record its history. His perspective is distorted by his limited knowledge, prejudice and ambition. He mentions the butler only in passing. The real author's perspective is obviously the more accurate because he is the creator; he views things from the outside. So does God, and so must we. History will look very different in the light of eternity. We will see that history is largely shaped by common disciples, not great leaders.

The Sage talked about a common man, a janitor, who shaped history from a biblical point of view. We will follow his example, not if we try to shape history directly, as most do, but if we are faithful to Jesus Christ. As it turns out, true fame will never come if we strive for it; it will only come if we obey God.

Study Questions
1. What is history's main drama?
2. In Joshua 1:1-8 God reveals to Joshua his destiny. How do you think this helped Joshua to complete his task?
3. According to Revelation 21 what is our destiny? How should this affect our lives now? How does it help to know God's plan?
4. What do you think is your role in the drama of history? In what ways can we learn and fulfill our individual destinies?

Chapter 7

THE GREAT TRANSFORMATION

THE MOST MEMORABLE story the Sage ever told me came from an old Hindu proverb:

Once there was a tiger who thought he was a goat. His mother had died at his birth and his father had abandoned him shortly thereafter; he was left alone to die. He was saved, however, by a herd of goats who found him, adopted him and brought him up as a goat. He ate like a goat, walked like a goat, fought like a goat (with his head, of course) and bleated like a goat. The only problem was that he wasn't a goat. He was a tiger. It made for a very awkward situation.

One day a great she-tiger prowled into the clearing where the goats were feeding. When they saw her they immediately scattered like seeds in a gust of wind. The young tiger, however, was too busy choking down more grass to notice that the goats had fled for their lives. The tigress eyed him warily. She had never before met a tiger living with a herd of goats, nor had she ever seen a tiger eating grass. She thought he was very peculiar, not at all suited to be a goat. So she decided to do something about it.

First, she roared until the jungles shook. She thought the power of her voice would surely awaken in him the feeling of being a tiger. But he began to tremble all over; then, when he saw her great form, the likes of which he had never seen before, he fell over, stuck his legs straight into the air and tried to play dead.

The tigress was not easily defeated. She marched up to him and stared into his face. He was such a beautiful animal, she thought, with all the potential to be a noble tiger. She pawed and batted his face about, hoping to arouse in him the strength and dignity she knew he could have. But he only whimpered and began to cry.

So she opened her jaws as wide as she could, picked him up by the scruff of the neck and carried him a short distance to a placid stream. Perhaps, she thought, he would get the point if he saw his reflection in a pool of water. She dropped him on the bank, made him stare at her face, then held his head right over the water so that he could see his image in the stream—that is, if he dared to look. But he didn't. He was too frightened, and besides, he was shaking so hard that his reflection was only a blur.

The tigress had only one idea left. She carried him back to the clearing, dropped him there and disappeared into the jungle. A few moments later she returned with a dead animal in her mouth. She tore it open, thus exposing the raw meat, took a bite of it and thrust the remaining flesh at his feet. Then she gave a long and low growl, which sounded just impatient enough to let him know what she was thinking.

The young tiger was horrified. Never had he eaten raw meat. The thought of it, to say nothing of the sight of it, made him sick. He bleated weakly and, instead of eating the meat, took another mouthful of grass. The tigress growled again, this time more loudly. Still he didn't move an inch closer to the carcass.

Then she roared, and he knew that he had no choice. He pawed the raw meat for a while, looking first at the meat and then at the stern face of the tigress. Finally, holding his breath, he took a bite. It tasted even worse than he thought it would. He wanted so to run away, but he didn't dare, especially after she growled again. She pushed him to take another bite. And another.

Gradually, something began to happen. He felt somehow different—stronger perhaps, or bigger. He felt the blood run through his veins. His heart began to beat wildly. His eyes narrowed. His tail twitched. He licked his chops. He plunged his teeth into the last of the meat and swallowed it whole. He looked again at the tigress. And he understood.

Digging his claws into the earth, he threw back his great head and roared—weakly perhaps, but convincingly just the same. Then he sprang into the jungle with the tigress close behind.

*   *   *

Tiger-Making

We are tigers who have been living like goats. God wants to make us into tigers again. God plans to shape us into new persons, stately, gracious and powerful. We are to take on the worthy stature we were destined to have. That is one of the directions discipleship takes.

God has told us clearly. He created us with the capacity to be like him. He intended us, right from the beginning, to be noble people: "Then God said, 'Let us make man in our image, after our likeness; and let them have dominion over the fish of the sea, and over the birds of the air, and over the cattle, and over all the earth, and over every creeping thing that creeps upon the earth' " (Gen 1:26).

The fall of the human race, as told in the story of Adam and Eve's temptation, deposed us from our position of eminence. We became twisted, rebellious, obsessed with ourselves. The image—our God-likeness—was seriously damaged but not beyond repair. From Genesis 12 through the book of Revelation the Bible tells the story of how God is rebuilding us into new persons so that his "likeness" can once more manifest itself in our lives. The stories of Abraham, Moses, Esther and others give examples of what God has in mind for all of us.

Jesus Christ proves just how serious God is. Christ's Incarnation, exemplary life and sacrificial death point the way toward a total reworking of human life. As we shall see in chapter ten, Christ is the one who repairs the damage in our relationship with God and also shows us, in his own life, what God wants us to be. Christ is the "first fruits" of creation. He is the image of the new person we can become.

The Scriptures refer to this divine intention time and again. This is not some minor subplot; this truth is at the heart of our faith: "And we all, with unveiled face, beholding the glory of the Lord, are being changed into his likeness" (2 Cor 3:18; see also Rom 8:29; 1 Jn 3:2).

C. S. Lewis understood this very well. In *Mere Christianity* he writes:

On the other hand, you must realize from the outset that the goal towards which He is beginning to guide you is absolute perfection; and no power in the whole universe, except you yourself, can prevent him from taking you to that goal. That is what you are in for. . . . We may be content to remain what we call ordinary people; but He is determined to carry out a quite different plan. To shrink back from that plan is not humility; it is laziness and cowardice. To submit to it is not conceit or megalomania; it is obedience.[11]

God is determined, as Lewis says, to make us like him. God's drama for history seizes the stuff of human life and enlarges it to fill divine dimensions. Thus discipleship has a direction. God plans to make us new persons.

This will affect who we are, what we believe in, how we think and what we do. For example, God will transform who we are. He will ennoble our *characters* by cultivating in us positive qualities that will help us to rise above inhospitable circumstances. The Bible calls these the fruit of the Spirit: unself-conscious concern for others, single-minded devotion to God, restfulness in God's sovereignty, an eye to see the best in others and energy directed into worthy causes. Further, he will shape what we believe. He plans to build in us *convictions* so that when we face pressure we will not compromise. Such convictions—a firm belief in marriage, a resolve to stay single for the sake of service, love for our enemies, devotion to the poor—form a foundation for integrity and fruitfulness. God will also influence our thinking by imparting to us *wisdom*, which is the integration of biblical knowledge and life experiences. Wisdom enables us to comprehend the universal principles that govern life. Finally, God's plan will affect what we do. He summons us to fulfill certain life *callings*. These are visions of what ought to be, and they are awakened by the ugliness of what is. Callings keep us from being limited by occupations. Occupations make us garbage collectors; callings will motivate us to beautify a city. Occupations make us insurance salespersons. Callings enable us to help others be good stewards of talents, resources, time and money. Occupations make us politicians. Callings send us to Washington with a vision of peace and justice.

Transformation
Becoming new persons, however, will not make us any less ourselves. If anything, we will become more ourselves. This is why I prefer to use the word *transformation* rather than the word *change*. Change implies a substitution. It denotes, according to Webster, "a making or becoming distinctly different." Transformation, on the other hand, implies an alteration in form, not substance. It allows for strong continuity. We transform clothes by dyeing them, cleaning them or repairing them. But we change clothes by throwing off one set for another.

God transforms. He made us the way we are; hence he will not change what we are in the most basic sense. Our personalities (talkative?), our aptitudes (musical?), our interests (the outdoors?) he will purify, break and rebuild, but not change. He sees nothing evil in who we are or what we can do. But he does see evil in how we flaunt our personalities and exploit our abilities. That is what he intends to address, like a surgeon attacking a malignant tumor to save the healthy organs threatened by it.

God loves a humorous person, but he hates base humor. He transforms funny persons by purifying their jokes, not by making them boring. Likewise, he loves the thinker, but he detests arrogance. He transforms brilliant people by making them humble, not stupid. Further, God loves our idiosyncrasies, but he hates those peculiarities that lead to snobbery. He transforms us by giving us self-control, not by erasing the delightful differences between us.

We need not fear that God will change us so totally that we will not be ourselves anymore. He does not want us to feel like strangers to ourselves or to pretend to be someone we cannot be. Rather, he purposes to transform us. When he is finished, we will feel compelled to applaud what he has done, for we will be totally and naturally ourselves. C. S. Lewis comments on this:

> The more we get what we now call ourselves out of the way and let Him take over, the more truly ourselves we become. There is so much of Him that millions and millions of "little Christs", all different, will still be too few to express Him fully. He made them all. He invented—as an author invents characters in a novel—all the different men that you and I were intended to be. In that sense our real selves are all waiting for us in Him. . . . It is when I turn to Christ, when I give myself up to His personality, that I first begin to have a real personality of my own. . . . The very first step is to try to forget about the self altogether. Your real, new self will not come as long as you are looking for it; it will come when you are looking for Him. [12]

In fact, becoming like Jesus Christ, far from depriving us of our identity, actually establishes strong self-identity. Christ enables us to find ourselves. Thus, as long as we avoid him and resist becoming like him, we will fail to discover our true selves. What we call "being ourselves" will turn out to be the worst kind of self-conscious conformity to the narrow standards of popular culture. Our "identity" will become the target for a fusillade of fads, popular opinions and unexpected circumstances. Our appearance will be conformed to the false faces on magazine covers. Our bodies will be compared to the measurements of a few sex gods and goddesses. Our minds will naively follow the latest intellectual craze. We will become the product of forces acting on us, and these will make us just like everybody else. Dare we call this "being ourselves"?

The Way of Death

The process of transformation, however, demands our death. We must die to become like Christ. We must die to live, lose ourselves to find ourselves, renounce what we have to inherit the world (Lk 9:23-26). The whole notion of becoming new persons is so utterly preposterous, so far beyond reasonable imagination, that only by dying to the idea of ever achieving it will we ever receive it. It is God's plan. It must be his doing, not ours.

Jesus used the example of a seed to explain why we must die (Jn 12:24-26). An oak seed contains the potential for becoming an oak tree, but it will remain a seed until it is planted and dies. If that seed could talk, we could imagine it saying something like, "Please don't plant me. I don't want to die. I am very happy being a seed." Fifty years later that same seed, now grown into an oak, would bless the farmer who planted it. The seed must die to become what it was meant to be. So must we.

We can understand why the requirements of discipleship stagger the mind. We always get more than we bargain for. Initially we embraced the Christian faith for a particular reason. We felt guilty, anxious or timid, and we found forgiveness, peace or confidence in the gospel. We all entered the Christian life through one of its many doors. But the door through which we walked is only the beginning. We found forgiveness, but God intends to make us forgiving. We discovered peace, but God sends us into the tumult. We gained confidence, but God commands us to be servants. God keeps pushing us farther than we ever wanted to go. He will push us all the way to Christlikeness.

This is why Jesus advised us to count the cost. God is planning to turn us inside out. Not one cell, muscle or bone in our bodies, not one second of our time, not one relationship, not one thought, not one decision will go untouched. Perhaps the oak seed wanted only to be a little bush; perhaps we want only to be nice, proper people. But the seed's desires, and ours, are really quite insignificant. It is a towering oak or nothing, Christlikeness or nothing. There is no middle ground.

Our transformation will therefore be total, not partial. God's designs are both magnificent and sobering. Nothing is left for ourselves, not even the crumbs of selfish motives. Any thought of stingy religious obligation is erased by God's calling to discipleship. He will not listen to our pleas for the leftovers. Real happiness in life is not gained from what remains after God has taken his share. God does not allow us to divide life into "religious" and "other." God will not give us Saturday night if we give him Sunday. We cannot relish the minor sins if we repent of the major ones. We cannot keep the mind for ourselves if we give him our hearts. He will keep demanding more of us. Indeed, he must. As Christ is inexhaustible, so is Christlikeness. It encompasses the whole of life; for we were made for it. God does not therefore demand something *from* us. What he wants is us.

Likewise, our transformation will be supernatural, not natural. We cannot become like Christ by mere human effort. Self-improvement efforts accomplish little by themselves. God does not want to make us better; he wants to make us new. Many of us think that kingdom living is like climbing a mountain. It is all labor and little rest; it is one careful step after another. But God does not want us to climb that mountain. He knows that we will surely fail. He plans to get us to the top another way, by giving us wings. As we shall learn later, God gives us grace (chapter twelve) and the Holy Spirit (chapter eleven) to lift us to the heights he wants us to reach.

Incredibly, this entire plan of making us like Christ is already accomplished. "If any one is in Christ, he *is* a new creation; the old has passed away, behold, the new has come" (2 Cor 5:17). Christ has given us an eternal destiny; and even now he is dwelling in our hearts. We will become like Christ, then, in the same way an adopted child is destined to exhibit the graces of the family to which he belongs. He is *already* a member of the family by his adoption, however contradictory his behavior is. The rest of life is a matter of learning to act differently, until his stature catches up with his status. God commands us, therefore, not to earn something he has already given, but to close the gap between his gracious action and our daily experience. In Jesus Christ we have the honored *position* of being God's adopted children. But we are also in a *process* of becoming new persons. We must strive now to live worthily of the status we have been given.

Finish then thy new creation,
Pure and spotless let us be;
Let us see Thy great salvation
Perfectly restored in Thee:
Changed from glory unto glory,
Till in heaven we take our place,
Till we cast our crowns before Thee,
Lost in wonder, love, and praise.[13]

Study Questions

1. Read 2 Corinthians 5:16-17. What does it mean, in your mind, to be a new person in Christ?

2. What is the relationship between *being* a new person in Christ and *striving* to live like Christ?

3. Read Genesis 1:26-27. What do you think it means to be made in God's image? How did the Fall affect this (Gen 3)?

4. What do 2 Corinthians 3:17-18 and Romans 8:28-30 teach about the goal of the Christian life?

5. In becoming like Christ—the goal of the Christian life—we will inevitably take on certain qualities. What do you think it means to have character? convictions? wisdom? life purpose?

6. How can you cultivate these in your life?

Chapter 8

A NEW
COMMUNITY
OF LOVE

SLOW-PITCH SOFTBALL was my idea of a great way to spend a lazy summer day. Our church team was one of eight from the small towns near our cottage. We squared off against each other on Tuesday and Thursday nights for what resembled an unholy war. It was the one time during the week when Christian behavior could be publicly compromised without having to endure the wrath of the church fathers and mothers. The only people who strongly disapproved of our combative manners were the umpires, who were the objects of a great deal of friendly insult and abuse.

During the summer I met the Sage, I played second base on a team that had the potential for a pennant. We were strong at the plate and agile on the field. Our only weakness was that we too often lost our tempers and with them the game, especially when we played the Free Will Baptists. They affronted us because they never said a word—no swearing, no insults, no jeers. They simply took to the field and beat everyone.

When we played them for the first time, they were in first place, with a 7 and 0 record, and we were in second, with a 6 and 1 record. Although I hesitated to take the Sage along with me, I decided that it would be culturally instructive for him to watch a softball game between two opposing churches. Differences in doctrine, of course, had nothing to do with it. We Lutherans simply didn't like the Free Willers.

"Ever been to a church softball game between Baptists and Lutherans?" I asked the Sage as we drove to the game.

"Yes, I once played on a team when I lived in Pennsylvania. I was a Baptist then. Why do you ask?"

"Oh, I just wanted to know if you knew what to expect."

"Just a friendly game. At least that's what you told me."

"Of course. Although sometimes it gets a little intense. I mean, there's nothing wrong with wanting to win, is there?"

"I suppose not," he said, smiling suspiciously.

When we arrived my teammates were already warming up. I pointed the Sage toward a clump of Lutherans who were sitting in the stands; then I joined my teammates and began to loosen up. I was soon lost in conversation. We began to discuss our strategy for the game, decided on a batting order, and challenged each other to play our best. A few of my teammates also vented their opinions about our opponents, whom they considered to be obnoxious, self-righteous and tough to beat. It would be humiliating, they said, to lose to such a group of holier-than-thous. Max, our big left fielder and the team's home run hitter and de facto leader, said that he wanted to annihilate them. As he spoke, his huge chest heaved; he sucked in his massive belly (enlarged by too many beers); his stare, aided by his dark eyes and thick eyebrows, was icy and cruel.

When the game was about to begin we discovered that our in-field umpire had not shown up. After inquiring into his whereabouts, we learned that he had fallen sick at dinner and would not be able to come. A few minutes later it was announced over the loudspeaker that they were looking for someone who could replace him. My teammates and I, assuming that the problem would be solved, took to the field for practice.

It was only after I heard "batter up" that I noticed who had volunteered. There stood the Sage, looking very serious and official, surveying the members of both teams with a wary eye. When our gazes met, I indicated surprise, but he remained expressionless, one of the few times that he ever did. My heart sank. I began to expect the worst.

The first inning, thank goodness, went quickly—two fly balls to the center fielder and a grounder to first. On the way to the dugout I stopped to talk with him.

"Why are you umping?" I asked nervously.

"Someone had to," he said.

"But why you? Have you done this before?"

"Does it matter? You're the one who told me that it was nothing but a friendly game among Christians. You said that I shouldn't take it too seriously."

"Well, it does matter. This is an important game. We don't like losing to these Baptists."

I ran over to our dugout where I had to answer a battery of questions about the Sage: Who was he? Could he actually see? Was he experienced?

"He'll be a pushover," Max said. "Let's heckle him, and if he makes a bad call, let's jump all over him. We'll have him on our side by the third inning."

My heart sank. I didn't know what to say or do, since I felt divided in my loyalties. So I said nothing. I knew the Sage was going to have a tough night.

For five innings the Sage tolerated minor insults, jeers and bad language without batting an eye. If anything, he seemed oblivious to it all. But then again, there were no close calls, nor had the game taken on the intensity I had anticipated.

All that changed in the sixth. The score was tied 2 to 2; the Baptists were at the plate; there were two outs and the bases were loaded. My teammates were noisier than ever, and our opponents, with eyes narrowed and conversation subdued, were seeing their chance to run away with the game.

Their hitter lined the first pitch to our third baseman who, miraculously, knocked the ball down, scrambled for it and threw a bullet to first. The Sage, with a great deal of certainty and vigor, called the runner safe. It was a close play.

My teammates exploded. Max steamed over from left field to give the Sage a piece of his mind. I will not repeat everything he said. Soon the entire team had surrounded and was yelling at him. They looked like a lynching party.

"Why don't you go back to a nursing home where you belong?"

"You couldn't see a softball if it were held in front of your nose."

"Are you a Baptist or something?"

This lasted for a couple of minutes. Then Max, still enraged, kicked some dirt on the Sage and cursed at him. The Sage turned and, flashing his eyes at Max, said, "You're out of this game."

We were stunned.

"What?" Max screamed.

"You're out. You've got ten seconds to get off this field or your team will forfeit the game."

The two of them stared at each other. I shall never forget the shocked face of Max and the bold eyes of the Sage. Max knew he was beaten. He turned and stomped off the field. We, too, turned from the Sage and resumed our positions, now totally deflated. We lost the game 10 to 3.

On the drive home we were silent for a while. Finally I could tolerate it no longer.

"Well, at least you've got guts," I said.

"I've met people like Max before," he replied. "In fact, I used to be as cocky as he is, only I had less size and strength to back me up. He's an intimidating fellow."

"That's not the word for it. He scares the heck out of me. So why did you throw him out?"

"Max wasn't the only problem. He was just the worst. It was, well, the whole group. You were like a mob."

"Or a lynching party?"

"You had the potential. I had to do something to break the momentum, to mitigate the power. So I kicked him out. Was I wrong?"

"I don't know. All I know is that I hate losing to Free Willers."

"Winning is that important?"

"I suppose not. Not when I'm alone, anyway. But the stakes get higher when I'm with the team."

"The mob again."

"Just a little friendly competition, that's all," I said with a smile.

*   *   *

Following the Herd

Groups have a power, both positive and negative, that individuals do not have. That is why when we participate in groups we often take on a group personality. We want to belong to a group in order to mitigate the problem of being a finite individual in what appears to be an enormous world. The small trickles of our lives risk evaporation unless we merge with others, thus becoming mighty rivers that carve out a permanent place in the universe. A group promises transcendence, and for that reason it has a power which no individual has. Once formed, it wields incredible power over individuals. Observe, for example, the behavior of teen-agers at a rock concert. Or consider otherwise sane adults at an athletic event. Or weigh the tacit brutality of millions of German citizens during Hitler's rise to power.

Such is the power of a group. It can drive us to evil—to take drugs, to injure others, to vandalize valuable property, to mock outcasts. It can make us do things we would never consider doing alone. Conversely, a group can push us to greatness—to protest an ugly war, to march against the evils of racism, to set a new record. In either case the influence of the group makes us go to the extreme. What we would never do by ourselves we readily do in a group.

We know this all too well. I suspect we would probably not dare to count the occasions when we have acted differently, usually for the worse, around a crowd of people. Language, once pleasant, becomes vulgar. Humor, once light-hearted, becomes unkind. Other people, once friends, become the butt of cruel jokes. As I learned at that church softball game, what would normally be aberrant behavior becomes accepted and even encouraged under the pressure of a group. Sometimes it takes the jarring words of someone like the Sage or the death of someone like Jesus to show us the terrible truth. Conflict between personal integrity and group acceptance usually leads to a sacrifice of the former, rarely the latter. A group has that kind of influence over individuals. It usually makes us worse, occasionally makes us better, but never leaves us the same.

In the last chapter we explored the first step in God's plan to reclaim the world. God wants to make us new persons. But he also knows that we are social beings, created to belong to a community of people. He purposes therefore to establish a *new community* to reverse the insidious group pressure that has made man's corporate life in the world so evil.

A New Israel

The foundation for the new community lies in the Old Testament. God called Abraham, and through his descendents God formed a nation, Israel. He shaped the character of this nation by the adversity they suffered in Egypt. Then he released them from their bondage, led them forth in power and commanded them to be a holy people. They were the recipients of God's favor. He made a "distinction" (Ex 11:7) between them and the other nations. Yet he also charged them to show mercy to the sojourner and to be a light to the nations. To reach a distant and prodigal world, therefore, God formed a new nation to show what he intends all peoples and nations to become. His own people were thus commanded to be different, as the last commandments of the Decalogue implied: fidelity, not adultery; service, not stealing; respect for life, not murder; loyalty, not lying; contentment, not covetousness. Such was the foundation for a new order of life.

This theme reached its pinnacle in the New Testament. Jesus called twelve disciples to form a new Israel. He intended them to be a new community of love. The early church obviously took Jesus' words seriously. The devotion of the first Christians to each other attracted the attention of the unbelieving world (Acts 2:42-47), causing the church to grow rapidly.

The apostle Paul taught that the goal of this new community is maturity in Christ (Eph 4:11-16). Such maturity both requires and creates unity. Jesus himself said that he would be satisfied with nothing less than perfect oneness. He prayed that the unity among Christians would reflect the oneness of the Father and the Son (Jn 17:20-23). Since the perfection of love is in God, he said that we would approach that perfection only when we love one another (Jn 15:12). Thus we are to have a special relationship with those who are of the household of faith (Gal 6:10).

There is a good reason for this. A community of love creates an environment in which God is free to work and people are free to respond. It affirms the best in us. It makes the Christian community a true body of believers, an organism, and it prepares the way for our ministry in the world. Jesus taught that our love for one another and the environment it establishes would confirm the integrity of our discipleship (Jn 13:34-35) and the divine origin of Jesus' ministry (Jn 17:20-26).

In fact, it is almost impossible to live as disciples without participating in a community of disciples. The pressure to accommodate to culture is too great if we live autonomously. Christian community encourages Christian obedience. If anything, when functioning properly the church actually reverses the cultural pressure: the world begins to see what it could and should be. Love challenges, convicts, attracts. The new community invites others to be disciples.

So profound is the love the new community possesses and imparts that it breaks down all barriers. Paul argued that the church should be inclusive. He perceived the mystery of God's will, that Jews and Gentiles, enemies for generations, are now fellow heirs and members of the same body. Christ has broken down the dividing wall of prejudice and self-righteousness which separated them (Eph 2:11-22). With the crumbling of that wall of hostility, all other walls fell too: between black and white, male and female, rich and poor, Marxist and capitalist.

Scripture also clarifies the responsibilities of those participating in the new community. Oneness requires that we make common commitments to keep the parts of the body of Christ connected together, as joints and ligaments do in the human body (Eph 4:16; Col 2:19). The Bible commands us, therefore, to admonish one another, forbear with one another, pray for one another, encourage one another and bear one another's burdens. Obedience to these reciprocal commands creates a bond among the members of the church, even among those different from ourselves.

But we must also welcome diversity. Again Paul used the example of human anatomy to prove his point. The church is like a body, having many parts. Every member has a necessary function to fulfill and a unique gift to share. Further, every member is dependent on all the rest. Thus Christians should have the confidence to give to others and the humility to receive from others. Diversity implies that we can reflect the fullness of Christ only corporately, not individually. Without the contributions of others we will inevitably develop blind spots in our character, heresy in our theology and imbalance in our ministry.

A Loyalty That Heals

The health and growth of the new community depends largely on the loyalty we demonstrate to each other—not the kind of one-sided and mindless loyalty of cult devotees, but the healthy loyalty which encourages both vulnerability and confrontation. It is the loyalty that should rouse us to listen to, challenge, struggle with, argue against and embrace each other. It is the kind of loyalty a husband and wife should have for each other. In public they always defend each other as if neither had a fault. In private they battle until their disagreements are resolved.

Such loyalty was portrayed in the movie *Spartacus*. After the defeat of his army by the Romans, Spartacus and hundreds of his followers were captured and sentenced to die. The prisoners were promised life, however, if only one of them would point out Spartacus, since the Roman generals had never met the man whose slave revolt had almost stormed into Rome itself. At this point in the movie they were scattered over a hillside, bound in chains, destined to die, silent and still. Finally, just as Spartacus was about to stand up to identify himself, another man jumped to his feet and said, "I am Spartacus." Then another announced, "I am Spartacus"; then another and another—until every man said the same words, thus sealing his fate. They were all crucified.

This kind of *other*-centered loyalty will do three things for us. First, it will protect us from the arrogance of using another Christian's faults, ambition and conceit to excuse our own. It will discipline us to be humble and keep us from reacting against the excesses we see in others. Loyalty will prevent conservatives, liberals, charismatics, evangelicals, mainliners, revolutionaries and everyone else from becoming caricatures of themselves.

Second, it will force us to be open to those whom we need the most but like the least. We usually tend to associate with people who, being like ourselves, buttress our beliefs and prop up our narrow perspectives. Moreover, we often avoid the people who, being different from us, are most capable of enlarging our minds and characters. Thus liberals and conservatives elude each other. Traditionalists and feminists dodge each other's view. Baptists and liturgical types have each other pegged. Creationists and evolutionists refuse to listen to each other. Evangelists and social activists reject each other's contributions. In shunning the company of people different from ourselves, we often become the victims of our own theological and personal blind spots. Only people with fresh perspectives can make us squirm and subsequently grow.

Third, loyalty will enable us to see people differently, and it will motivate us to invest ourselves in them. It will force us to look beyond appearance, intellect, background, culture and even theology to the person within. It will give us a different set of eyes. We will begin to see that the stupid and incompetent people we normally pass over for appointments and honors have the capacity to become noble creatures, while the confident, attractive, popular and able people who get all our attention have the capacity to be ugly and selfish. God does not judge a person by outward appearance and ability; instead, he perceives what is in the heart (1 Sam 16). It is ultimately the heart that determines the quality of our lives, whether we will become small or great. Thus God commands that we see all people—the prisoner, the black, the white, the square, the artistic, the unusual, the ordinary—as he sees them and that we then encourage them to grow toward their greater destiny. Loyalty builds bonds among Christians so that we can perceive and nurture the capacities we all have for Christlikeness.

The new community, therefore, reverses the pressure of group behavior that often draws the worst out of people. It creates an environment in which Jesus can rule and Christians can grow. It engenders love so that we can see the best in others and become the best ourselves.

Study Questions
1. Have you ever been swayed by a group to do something you didn't want to do? Why did you do it?
2. The church, when functioning properly, creates an environment encouraging discipleship. In 1 Corinthians 12:12-26, what do we learn about how the church functions best?
3. The Bible suggests two ways of demonstrating loyalty to other Christians: establishing oneness and using gifts. What do we learn about creating unity in Hebrews 10:24-25 and Galatians 6:2?
4. What do we learn about the gifts of the Spirit in Romans 12:3-8?
5. What is one specific way you can create unity with other Christians? How can you use your gift for others?

Chapter 9

VISION FOR
THE NEW WORLD

THE SURVIVAL OF THE fittest," the Sage said under his breath.

"What?" I asked, surprised by this interruption of our Sunday afternoon stroll. When I turned to look at him, I saw that he was staring at a huge maple tree that stood in a clearing just off to our right.

"That maple tree," he said, now fully aware of me, "has beaten all of its competitors. Now it's like some aged warrior living off the fruits of its victories. Look at the size of that giant!"

He wasn't exaggerating. I'd never noticed the sheer bulk of that tree before, although I had walked by it a dozen times. It towered above the rest of the trees in the woods.

"Survival of the fittest," I said. "That's from Herbert Spencer, I think. We studied his ideas in biology class. But what does he have to do with this maple tree?"

"This one maple tree," he said, "has battled all kinds of forces—competition for sun, minerals and water, inhospitable weather, human encroachment, fire, the advance of time, and it still survives."

"You make it sound as if that tree actually *tried* to survive—I mean, that it *worked* at it."

"In a sense, I think it did. Consider this"—he stared for a moment at the tree—"in plants and animals alike there seems to be a kind of will to survive. Living things learn to adapt, and when they must die, as all living things do, they always produce another generation to follow them. It's really quite fascinating."

"Why?" I asked.

"Because most species work very hard just to reproduce another generation. They resist the constant threat of death by passing on something of themselves to their offspring. It's a violent business, once you learn about it. Plants, insects, fish, mammals—all struggle and even die to reproduce another generation. I think nature has a longing to preserve itself. Perhaps it's looking for better days and wants to survive until it gets there."

We walked along the path for a while without exchanging words or glances.

"Now I have a question for you," he said. "Is what I just talked about true for humans? Do we have a will to survive? Are we looking for better days?"

I thought about it for a few minutes. I knew that I wanted to survive. And death? I wanted nothing to do with it. But why do people die heroically? It must be to preserve their society and protect the next generation. "Women and children first," I said to myself. Of course, they represent the hope of the future. But if it's all that simple, why do we build such complex societies? I had no answer to that question.

"Yes, we're looking for better days," I said. "But it's still too simple. I mean . . . why is life so complicated then?"

"Because we humans have the capacity," he said, "not only to survive in anticipation of better days but also to create the better days we long for. That's how culture is formed. We want to build something permanent.

"I remember," he said, "once watching a crew of men building one of the towers of the World Trade Center in New York City. I was entranced by their work. At their break I asked several of the men what they were doing. Most of them said that they were making money or, more cynically, that they were building another eyesore for New York's already overcrowded skyline. But one man, a Puerto Rican as I remember, said that he was helping to erect a masterpiece of engineering. Another explained to me the difficulty of erecting skyscrapers. They were obviously proud to be a part of the project. 'This will be a famous building some day,' the first one said to me. 'My children will remember me when they see it; they will say, "My father, Alberto, worked on this great structure." ' "

The Sage looked at me.

"To me life doesn't become real life," he said, "until a person decides, as that man did, to invest his life in something greater than himself."

*   *   *

Better Days

Something is amiss in the world, and everyone knows it. We see potential in the world for beauty, greatness, even perfection. That is why many of us are so troubled by the lack of greatness and the glaring imperfection and ugliness that surround us. That is also why we work so hard to try to repair and restore our broken world. Underneath the coats of crusty paint and discolored varnish is pure, stately oak. We know it is there. We want to strip off the ugly stuff and start all over.

The Sage mentioned that the creation *longs for* survival and for "better days." The whole universe seems to be crying out for pres-ervation and perfection. "There must be something more than this," it sighs before the specter of death. "We were not born to die." We humans, however, can do more than merely survive. We can renovate, transform, reshape. We are able to build a culture in which buildings, institutions, monuments, ideas, art and technology outlive us. We humans stand alone. We *believe* the world is meant to be a better place and strive to make it that way.

We therefore cannot understand the world rightly unless we see its potential for perfection juxtaposed against its present sordid condition. The Bible teaches that there is a sharp difference between the way things are and the way they were meant to be. God created Adam and Eve to live together blissfully in the garden of Eden, where they were destined to reign over the natural world. Their lust for equality with God, however, deposed them from their lofty position. They became separated from God. Their sin fractured the intimacy they had with each other (Gen 3:8). Even their life in the natural world turned wretched (Gen 3:16-19). Adam had to sow and harvest his grains and fruits with the sweat of his brow; Eve had to bear her children in pain.

The rebellion poisoned their offspring, too. Cain murdered Abel but denied any responsibility for it (Gen 4). Later, even the imaginations of the thoughts of people turned utterly corrupt (Gen 6:5). Finally, after the great flood, an ambitious king urged an entire society to build a tower into the heavens and so "make a name" for itself, thus causing the very structures of society to compete against God. Culture itself, as represented later by Sodom, Babylon and Rome, tried to make the rule of God unnecessary. It still does.

So the world has become a baleful, tortured place. Such a state is bitter to us because we feel a sense of loss, as if the world were a famous physician now living as a drunkard on skid row. It is still possible to spot vestiges here and there of what it was meant to be. A trip to the mountains or a dip in a pure stream make littered highways and polluted rivers more odious to us. Architectural wonders and manicured parks only accent the ugliness of ghettos and cemented cities. An occasional encounter with a polite sales clerk or pleasant dealings with a reliable business underline the rude behavior of many people and the greedy policies of many enterprises.

Perhaps we have even tried, as have all generations, to make the world a better place. We want the rivers to be clear again, the buildings to be new, the institutions of society to be our servants and not our lords. We march and legislate, comfort and challenge, scrape and paint, sow and harvest, but still the darkness closes in on us. And in time we discover that the enemy is not only in society; it is also in us. We, too, are part of the problem.

Rebuilding Jerusalem

Our longings for renewal draw attention to and anticipate the great work that God wants to do. As he plans to make us new persons and to establish a new community, he also wants to build a new world, out of the very stuff of the old one. The world belongs to God. He will not be satisfied until he reclaims it and restores it to what he intended it to be. The Christian faith is like a drama because we have been summoned by God to participate in this reclamation process.

The Scriptures use several images to outline the extent of this reclamation. In Romans 8:21 we read, "The creation itself will be set free from its bondage to decay and obtain the glorious liberty of the children of God." Creation yearns for the same thing we do—a new world. Further, the Scriptures employ the image of the city, not only to underscore the depths of the Fall (Lk 19:41-44; Gen 11) but also to sketch the social dimensions of God's final triumph in the coming of the new Jerusalem, the holy city (Rev 21:1-2). True salvation encompasses both man *and* his social environment.

Still, we are left with a problem. We live closer to Sodom and Nineveh, Rome and Corinth, Detroit and Calcutta, than we do to the new Jerusalem. If we do belong to the kingdom of God, it is an unseen, unnoticed, often unknown kingdom. Where is this new world the Bible talks about?

Jesus understood the problem, and he addressed it by using parables. First, he talked about how to respond to evil in the world. The kingdom of God, he said, can be compared to a field of new growth which an enemy pollutes by sowing weeds in it. Thus the wheat ripens in an impure field, and it is impossible to separate the wheat from the weeds until the harvest (Mt 13:24-30). Jesus was saying that we should expect good and evil to exist side by side until he returns to judge and separate them. There is no perfection and purity to be found this side of eternity. We must learn, in the meantime, to represent the kingdom of God and to champion the cause of Christ even in a hostile environment. We are citizens of an invisible kingdom; but we are charged to establish it, however imperfectly, in the visible world.

Second, he explained how to have hope, even in the worst of circumstances. The kingdom of God is also like a mustard seed, one of the smallest of seeds, that grows into a large shrub (Mk 4:30-32). What therefore appears to be weak, fragile and powerless (and the kingdom of God does appear to be that way at times) will someday tower over the rest of the world. It is only a matter of time.

Third, he told his disciples how to function in society until he returns. The church, he said, is to be the *buffer* between the kingdom and the world. It should function in the world like salt, creating a thirst for God, preserving the larger society from rotting and drawing out the flavor of what culture, at its best, can be (Mt 5:13). As salt penetrates the substance on which it is shaken, so the church should penetrate society with good deeds. This implies that we should treat everything in the world as part of God's rightful domain. Since he wants to redeem all, we should envelop all with the creative, energetic love of God.

The Presence of the Future

We know, of course, that Christ will redeem the world totally only after he comes again to establish his kingdom on earth. In the meantime our efforts must *anticipate* his return, for there is a dynamic relationship between Christ's final triumph and our present service. Suppose you are the renter of an old, run-down house and you want to make improvements on it. Your cosmetic efforts (painting, repairs and the like) will not truly transform the house, for you lack the necessary capital and expertise to renovate it. But your efforts do invite and anticipate the more substantial work of the owner, who will subsume your cosmetic work into his remodeling.

Likewise, we are partners with God. Our kingdom work, however faltering and limited, points to his final work. In fact, the ultimate reclamation of the world (at the consummation) will integrate all that we have done, by faith, into all that God will do. The new heavens and the new earth will actually contain the fruits of our labors; only they will be perfected. Thus every building constructed to the glory of God will be a part of the new world; only there the steel will be changed to brass, the tile to marble, the veneers to true oak. The music composed to honor God will be sung or played in heaven; only there they will produce a sound we had hoped but failed to create. The people we nurtured will be with us in heaven; only there they will be complete. There is a continuity, then, between our present service and the final renewal.

We can hope for one thing—the kingdom's victory is inevitable. God's Word says it, and Christ's resurrection proves it. The resurrection is the link between our hope for renewal and our awareness of decay and death. It is the link between future and present, because it represents the future invading the present. Jesus was human, subject to all the limitations and burdens of being human. He even became the victim of death, the last and greatest enemy. Yet he rose from the dead and appeared before his disciples in bodily form. He was recognizable, the same Jesus they had known before. But he had a perfect body, fit to dwell in eternity and to reign over the universe. The resurrection of Jesus ensures that God's plan for the entire world will succeed. What God accomplished in creation, lost in the Fall, and initiated in the resurrection will be completely restored in the consummation. Christ is the first in the long line of wonderful renewals. His resurrected life is before us all, pointing the way. The rest is yet to come (1 Cor 15:23-24).

A New World Coming
Jesus warned us time and again (Mt 25; Mk 13) that since the

triumph of the kingdom is inevitable, then we must invest in that coming kingdom now. The Bible does not tolerate neutrality and double-mindedness. There is no middle ground. It is impossible to believe in the kingdom and not live for it.

We must therefore be *patient* and *persistent* in our labors. "Therefore, my beloved brethren, be steadfast, immovable, always abounding in the work of the Lord, knowing that in the Lord your labor is not in vain" (1 Cor 15:58). Regardless of the opposition, we must never capitulate to the lure of comfort and to the tyranny of the immediate. We must stay true to our callings, whether it be to our families in a culture encouraging unfaithfulness, or to a firm set of values in a corporate structure committed only to making profits, or to steady identification with the poor in a society that tries to ignore rampant poverty. We must believe that our efforts, when applauded *or* when rejected, will manifest the kingdom to the world.

We must also *discern* who the real enemy is as we struggle to build a new world. The enemy is not people, institutions, enterprises or movements, not ultimately anyway. However evil these appear to be, they represent goals that have been perverted by the real enemy, Satan. Passionate, judgmental opposition to these false enemies will only accelerate the process of alienation and moral deterioration which we are supposed to slow down and reverse. Further, it will delude us into thinking that if only we can eliminate *this* base person or *that* evil institution, we will usher in a Christian utopia. Such hopes deceive us. We should resist Satan and his insidious plans, but we should also reclaim what he has usurped (see chapter fifteen).

Finally, we must have a *vision* of the coming kingdom, in concrete, earthly terms. Such vision will compel us to study, to pray, to debate, to plan, until a picture of a new world emerges. "This is what life ought to be," we will say to ourselves. Such a vision will constrain us to action.

We have many examples of visionaries to inspire us. Prison Fellowship, founded by Watergate offender Charles Colson, has begun to redeem the penal system in our country. Too many Christians have identified its faults; too few have tried to change it. Likewise, while the evangelical wing of the church was still disparaging political careers, Mark Hatfield entered the maze of politics to effect Christian principles. World Vision and Bread for the World were established to arouse the Christian public to use the resources of this country, both material and political, to feed the hungry world. Martin Luther King, Jr., also had a vision.

I have a dream that one day on the red hills of Georgia the sons of slaves and the sons of former slaveowners will be able to sit down together at the table of brotherhood. . . . I have a dream that my four little children will one day live in a Nation where they will not be judged by the color of their skins, but by the conduct of the character. . . . I have a dream that one day every valley shall be exalted: every hill and mountain shall be made low, the rough places will be made plane, the crooked places will be made straight and the glory of the Lord shall be revealed and all flesh shall see it together.[14]

It is easy to critique; it is tough to restore. Reclamation requires a vision of what the world ought to be.

There is a new world coming, one that we can anticipate and even help to build *now* by how we live. So whatever our station in life—architect, homemaker, executive, student, laborer, contractor, writer—we must dare to envision what God intends to do in the world and believe that he will use us to accomplish it, at least in part. Discipleship will never make us content with personal security. It will press us to embrace the world God has made and wants to reclaim. "Thy Kingdom come, Thy will be done, on earth as it is in heaven."

Study Questions
1. What are some of the signs of the Fall we see around us? of the world's goodness?
2. Read Genesis 1:1—2:3. What do you learn about God's plan in creation?
3. What do Matthew 5:13-20 and 28:18-20 teach us about our present

responsibility in transforming the world?

4. What do you think it means to be committed to world reclamation?

5. What can you do *now*, considering your present location and resources, to be a part of God's great work of creating a new world?

Chapter 10

THE WAY
TO RENEWAL

THE VIETNAM WAR WAS raging out of control during my high school and early college years. I still remember the reports of two hundred or three hundred American soldiers being killed every week and the initiation of the draft lottery, a sophisticated form of Russian roulette. The mood of America slowly shifted from naive support to cogent criticism. The Sage and I discussed the war throughout the summer. I was interested, if for no other reason than that I feared the draft. The Sage, too, was interested, but for a different reason. He was aware of the social, political and economic implications of the war. He believed that the war had the potential of irreparably damaging the fragile unity of our nation.

It occurred to me one day that we had never actually talked about war itself, but only about the effects of war on American life.

I wondered if the Sage had ever seen real war.

"Ever been in the Army?" I asked him one day after noticing the headlines.

"No, not the Army," he said. "The Air Force."

"Really? During a war?"

"World War 2," he said.

"Did you ever see any action?"

"Fought on the Pacific front for a whole year."

"Doing what?"

"I was a navigator on a small bomber."

"Then you actually flew bombing missions?"

"Many," the Sage said. "We always cleared the way for the land troops when they were about to invade another island."

"Did any of your missions run into trouble?" I asked. "I mean, were you ever shot at?"

"Shot down," the Sage said.

"Shot down! You're kidding me."

"I wish I were."

"How did it happen?"

"We were on a mission over a small island in the Philippines. After dropping our bombs, we suddenly ran into a few Japanese fighters. Unfortunately, we were given no fighter support of our own. I guess the mission was too small to warrant it. We were like sitting ducks. We tried to hold them off but couldn't."

"So you were shot down," I said.

"Three of our planes were hit. The crews from two of them, including mine, were able to parachute to safety."

"Right into the water, I suppose."

"Unfortunately, yes," he said. "But we were near enough to an island to swim to it. Thank goodness we had life preservers."

"Was anyone hurt?"

"One man, the gunner, had been wounded in the air battle. We did our best to stop the bleeding; then we made our way toward the island."

"A friendly island, I hope."

"We weren't sure, but we doubted it. While still about a quarter mile out we spotted a couple of small fishing boats headed straight toward us. At first we thought it was the Japanese, but we soon discovered they were natives.

"After picking us up, they paddled along the coast until they came to a bay. Turning into it, we spotted a small village. They hid us there, fed us and cared for us. They were extraordinarily kind."

"Didn't the Japanese look for you?" I asked.

"They looked all right. But the natives played dumb. Surprisingly, it worked. I suspect the Japanese thought that even if we had survived, we would never be able to get off the island. The waters were regularly patrolled, especially around the villages. That created a problem. We had no idea how we could escape."

"So how did you?" I asked.

"On a more remote side of the island the natives had hidden a fishing boat. The Japanese rarely patrolled there. One night we left the village and made our way to that side of the island. To ensure our safety, a couple of natives dressed in our uniforms and went ahead of us. We learned later that one of them was shot and killed."

"Like decoys."

"Incredible, isn't it? That's getting into another person's skin."

"Did all of you make it?"

"Yes, we made it. Freedom never felt so good."

"Freedom to do what you wanted to do."

"No. Freedom to do what I knew I had to do: to live like the natives who risked their lives for us."

*　　　　*　　　　*

The Door to God

We have explored the direction of discipleship. God wants to make us new persons; he has established a new community; he is working to create a new world. This is God's promise. It is the drama of history.

But there is one last question we must ask and try to answer. We know what God wants to do. Now we must know how. How can we find *the way?* God's plan is so grandiose that it seems impossible to reach, beyond human attainment. How can we get there?

Jesus answered, "*I* am the way." If the Father offers all good things to us, he does so *through* the Son. Jesus is the link between God and us. He directs us toward our greater destiny. He makes the plan of discipleship possible, in spite of our weakness and blindness. And he does this in two ways. Christ is the way in that he is our mediator, and he is the way in that he is our example.

Jesus is the way we get to the Father and avail ourselves of the Father's promises. He makes us worthy to receive the gift of eternal life and to live in the presence of God. Christ mediates what God wants to give us, the destiny he has in mind for us. He is the perfect go-between, the ideal channel.

The Bible uses concepts of everyday life to explain this. It employs the terminology of the courtroom ("justification"), the marketplace and the slave auction ("redemption"), the sacrificial system ("propitiation" and "atonement"), the world of diplomacy ("reconciliation") and agriculture ("vine and branches"). Each concept carries different nuances, but the truths are one. Jesus Christ introduces us to the Father, repairs our broken relationship with him and thus enables us to receive the bounty of being his children. Jesus is the Way.

The Bible explains exactly how. In it we learn that God created us in his image, with the capacity to be like him, under the one condition that we be totally dependent on him. But someone with the capacity to be like God is also necessarily free. So we also had the capacity to become very much unlike God, horribly self-centered, greedy and proud. That is what happened to Adam and Eve, and the whole human race ever since. We have rejected God's design by denying his goodness and by trying, very unsuccessfully, to live independent of him. The consequences, both then and now, have been disastrous. We have almost succeeded in destroying ourselves.

Man's rebellion prevented God from fulfilling his real intention, to make us like himself. It left him with a horrible choice: to abandon his scheme and us with it, or to woo us back. We know that this dilemma was resolved in Jesus Christ. God decided to pursue the latter course, and it was a costly choice. He had two barriers to break down: our obstinacy and his justice.

It would have been convenient had God been able to pardon us with a simple gesture of forgiveness. But he was not able to do that. His justice prohibited such an easy solution. God's very character makes sin intolerable to him. He could no more dismiss our rebellion and still be God than a state could ignore crime and remain a just state. If a governing body tolerated crime, it would abrogate its responsibility, lose its authority and so encourage anarchy. If God tolerated sin, he would cease to be God. God is therefore not neutral about sin, nor is he casual in the way he deals with it. He hates sin, and he deals with it severely.

So to honor God and to rescue a stubborn people, Jesus came. The Son of God, the equal to the Father, was born a man to identify with humanity. He was eventually murdered by the very people he came to save, thus demonstrating how low the human race had descended and how desperately his own death was needed. Three days later, of course, he rose from the dead and became the "first fruits" of those who follow him.

Just so did Jesus repair our relationship with God by dying in our place. His sacrificial death invites us to yield to God just as it frees God to accept us. It provides a channel of love that flows two ways. Thus the way to become new persons, to establish a new community, and to create a new world is Jesus Christ. He is like the native who took up the Sage's clothes and put them on his own back. He did more than identify with us. He died for us so that we might live for and reign with God.

Following Jesus

Jesus is also the Way in that he is our example. The whole spirit of the Scriptures makes this impossible to overlook. Christ is *unique* in that he, as the Son of God, restored our life with God. But he is also our *model* in that he, as a man, learned obedience and lived by faith. Discipleship requires us to follow the example of Jesus.

Jesus himself said:

> Do you know what I have done to you? You call me Teacher and
> Lord; and you are right, for so I am. If I then, your Lord and
> Teacher, have washed your feet, you also ought to wash one
> another's feet. For I have given you an example, that you also
> should do as I have done to you. (Jn 13:12-15)

Peter confirmed this by writing:

> But if when you do right and suffer for it you take it patiently,
> you have God's approval. For to this you have been called, be-
> cause Christ also suffered for you, leaving you an example, that
> you should follow in his steps. He committed no sin; no guile
> was found on his lips. When he was reviled, he did not revile in
> return; when he suffered, he did not threaten; but he trusted
> to him who judges justly. He himself bore our sins in his body
> on the tree, that we might die to sin and live to righteousness.
> (1 Pet 2:20-24)

Peter's thought is perplexing here because he tells us to follow
Christ's example, but then he mentions an example, namely,
Christ's sacrificial death, which we could never imitate. Obviously
we must distinguish, then, between Christ's *example,* which we are
supposed to follow, and its *effects,* which are unique. We are commanded to wash one another's feet, in imitation of Christ, but the
fruits of Christ's act of humiliation will exceed our own, both in
kind and in degree. Likewise, we must suffer and even die for others, as Christ did, but his death will always be incomparable and
unrepeatable. We must follow the way of Christ; he is our example.
But it is a way he himself has established for us by his unparalleled
life, death and resurrection. Christ is both the only Son of God and
the accessible, albeit inexhaustible, image of what the human race
was meant to be.

Let's say that you are the president of a small college, and you
aim to be the best. So you begin searching for a model of excellence.
A few months later you meet the president of a huge university.
His reputation for excellence, you discover, is beyond question. You
therefore try to imitate his character, follow his style of manage-

ment, uphold his convictions and pursue his vision. In time you succeed and do exactly what he does. Yet the effects of his presidency, by virtue of the size and prestige of his institution, still far exceed your own. You imitate him, but he surpasses you. The analogy, of course, is not perfect. Christ not only accomplished more than we ever will; he also did something utterly unique, unrepeatable, unfathomable. His work was once for all.

Christ's example is so exacting that only by his power will we be able to conform to it. Thus we must, above all else, pursue him. He will burn his life into us. He will mediate divine life into our hearts. Thomas Merton writes,

> As a magnifying glass concentrates the rays of the sun into a little burning knot of heat that can set a fire to a dry loaf or a piece of paper, so the mystery of Christ in the Gospel concentrates the rays of God's light and fire to a point that sets fire to the spirit of man. And this is why Christ was born and lived in the world and died and returned from death and ascended to His Father in heaven. . . . Through the glass of His incarnation He concentrates the rays of His Divine Truth and Love upon us so that we feel the burn, and all mystical experience is communicated to men through the man Christ.[15]

Study Questions

1. Can you think of one or two people who have sacrificed for you? What did they do and how did you benefit?
2. The Bible teaches that Jesus makes us right with God. What do we learn about his mediating role in Romans 5:1-11?
3. The Bible also teaches that Jesus should be our example. What do we learn about this in John 13:12-17?
4. What specific struggles are you having right now and how is Christ working through them?
5. Can you think of particular ways in which you could better follow Christ's example in your life?

IV
DIVINELY POWERED
DISCIPLESHIP

Discipleship has a direction. God is in the process of building new persons, a new community and a new world. We must have power, however, if we want to progress in this direction. Human vitality and effort is not enough, so great is the destiny God has designed for us and so great is our human weakness. God's power is given to us through the Holy Spirit. Through the Spirit, God comes to live within us as an internal source of power (chapter eleven). Because of his mercy and love God also works externally in our lives, using events and circumstances for our good. Grace is the initiative God takes to shape our lives (chapter twelve). A third aspect of God's power, however, we hold in ourselves. It is the power of choice. Though we are not capable of changing ourselves into what God wants us to be, we can decide to respond to God's Spirit acting on us so that God can transform us (chapter thirteen). To begin, then, we must explore the person and work of the Holy Spirit. The Sage introduces us to the topic by describing a marriage that changed his life.

Chapter 11

REDISCOVERING
THE HOLY SPIRIT

I HAD HEARD THE WEEK before our first encounter that the Sage was divorced. Though he had indirectly verified the rumor on one or two occasions, we had never discussed it. I had forgotten about it until he brought it up one evening at the cottage.

We had just finished eating dinner with my parents and had retired to the porch to watch the sunset. The Sage, though still friendly, was more quiet and somber than usual. He seemed sad to me, reflective.

"Your parents have a good marriage," he said to me. "They love each other. I noticed that the moment I met them."

"Yes, I guess they do," I said. "I've not thought about it much."

"I certainly have," he said. "But then I'm sensitive to it in a way you can't be, at least not yet. I've learned that the decision to marry is momentous. Marriage changes your life permanently. And its effects can never be erased."

"I'm glad I'm single," I said. "I can't imagine being married."

"It's not easy being single," he said. "But it's not any easier being married. I wish I had known that before I got married." He paused, then continued, this time more pensively. "Did you know that I was married once?"

I nodded.

"And did you know I was divorced?"

"Someone told me you were," I said.

"It has been fifteen long years since our initial separation. You know, I still think about our marriage a great deal. It wields a strange power over me."

For a long time we were quiet as we watched the sun sink behind the clouds on the horizon. The play of sun, clouds and water, and the shifting shades of color created a kind of celestial dance on the horizon lasting until dusk. The whole scene entreated us to be silent and encouraged our reflection. For some reason, I knew that our conversation would continue, and I was right. The Sage fell into a monolog, as if he were allowing me to peer into his soul.

"During all my married years I met only one couple whose marriage was really attractive to me. Sadly, by the time my wife and I met them it was already too late, at least to save our marriage. He was a lawyer in New York City; she was an artist and homemaker. They had two children, both grown up. We first met them at a party for, if I remember correctly, a friend's twenty-fifth wedding anniversary. Gary was friendly in a, well, natural sort of way. His wife, Beth, had the same manner, only more quiet and intense. I hadn't met many people like them before.

"They took a surprising interest in us. I learned later that they sensed something was wrong between Sally and me. They wanted to see if they could help.

"The next week they invited us over for dinner. Predictably,

Sally and I argued all the way to their apartment. I can't even remember what it was about. We fought more out of habit than out of deep conviction. When we arrived, I was prepared, as usual, to impress our hosts and pretend that Sally and I were blissfully married. When they welcomed us into their home, however, I knew that something was different. You see, *they* didn't want to impress us. They were totally themselves.

"In twenty-five years of marriage I don't think we ever found the joy we felt that night by being with Gary and Beth. She was an unassuming hostess, he a lively listener, both compassionate friends. Even their problems, which they didn't try to hide, were engulfed by the larger dimension of the love they had in their home. Sally and I were caught up in something bigger and better than ourselves. It was, as I learned later, their marriage. Had we been able to spend more time with them, I think we could have resolved our differences and saved our marriage. They had that kind of power between them.

"The next day Sally filed for divorce. The previous night's engagement had given me hope, but it had driven her to despair. She could not even imagine having a marriage that good. Because she was an idealist, she refused to settle for less. So she gave up.

"I wasn't surprised, and I didn't really blame her, either. There had been too many late nights, too many insults, too many ambitious plans for fame, too many occasions when I was lured away by the promise of wealth, too many times of neglecting the children, who had become strangers to me.

"That night I marched into the den, sat in my favorite high-backed leather chair, smoked a cigar and drank ten martinis. I was half hoping that I would die, I was so desperate. The next day I called up Gary for help and thus began our deep friendship.

"For the next year or so I saw them at least once a week, and for two weeks, after I moved out of our apartment, I lived with them. At first I was attracted to them for the love and support I received *from* them, which was substantial and rarely reciprocated by me. Eventually, however, I grew to appreciate something else even more—their marriage. Their love for each other was unfathomable. It had a life all its own. It had a healing and renewing spirit to it. I breathed in that spirit, and it changed my life. They are the reason why I became a Christian."

*　　　*　　　*

Introducing the Holy Spirit

For many years after my conversion the Holy Spirit was a stranger to me. I had heard hundreds of sermons on every conceivable topic, except on the Holy Spirit. I knew as much about him as I knew about infralapsarianism. And what is that? I was familiar with the Trinitarian formulas of the creeds and thus knew that the Holy Spirit is the third person of the Godhead and that he was sent by Jesus to empower and enliven the first disciples. Beyond that, my knowledge dropped off sharply.

For a while I thought that the Holy Spirit was an "it," some kind of mystical force, the likes of which we read about only in fantasy stories. To tap its power, magic would do as well as faith. I also believed that the real power of the Spirit was reserved only for exceptionally religious people, and I was certainly not one of them. Religious television, of the more wild and demonstrative variety, persuaded me that I could use the Holy Spirit to get what I wanted, if only I could figure out how to get him (or it) under my control.

Later exposure to the charismatic movement stimulated my curiosity. The Holy Spirit had been "rediscovered," a famous speaker once said at a conference I attended. By the spirited atmosphere in the convention hall, presumably engendered by *the* Spirit, I knew that he was on to something. For once I heard someone explain the gifts of the Spirit systematically, and I participated in worship without feeling I was part of an audience watching a performance of preaching appended by a few preliminaries. I was drawn toward the life and thinking of this movement, and I am glad I was.

Still, I continued to be confused by other voices in the church, whose theologies were too narcissistic for me. The Spirit seemed to be subjected to the vicissitudes of human feelings and to the sensationalism of the miraculous. Why were tongues so necessary for assurance? Why did so many have to be "slain in the Spirit" to know the power of God? And why, I asked, did the miraculous gifts get more attention than the unassuming ones, like service and mercy? I grew tired of always having to feel the Spirit. I wanted to know him.

I suspect that you want to know him too. The liveliness of the early Christians is evidence enough of what the Holy Spirit can do. Yet their life in him was, with very few exceptions, natural and unself-conscious, much more than ours is. They simply received his life and power and then went about the business of being Christ's disciples. They did it very well. What knowledge did they have that we lack?

Discipleship requires power. The early church had this power, and it was the secret of their spiritual success. It can be for us, too, if we understand *who* the Holy Spirit is, *what* he does and *how* he works.

Who He Is

We cannot know the Holy Spirit unless we first know something about God; in particular, the relationship that exists within the Godhead, between the Father and the Son.[16] We say, "God is love," but what we really mean is "love is God," which of course is not a Christian statement at all. Love is no more God than romance *is* marriage or matter *is* life. God cannot be reduced to a personified version of what we think love is.

God is love, yes. That implies, however, that love exists within God himself. God must have someone to love besides what he created or he could not have been love before he created. God's love is not limited to the world, just as a father and mother's love is not limited to their children. Love requires an object. We never love in the abstract; we love persons. So does God. He loves within himself.

This introduces us to the heart of our Trinitarian faith. God is love because he is, in a mysterious way, a relationship. He is one;

yet he exists in three persons. Therefore God is able to love within himself. The Father loves the Son, infinitely and totally, and the Son loves the Father.

Thus God is a relationship. How is it possible, then, to conceive of this? Here we must venture into the world of classical theology. From the Council of Nicea (A.D. 325) on, theologians have distinguished between the meaning of two words, *making* and *begetting*, to explain this Trinitarian mystery. We *make* something when we use our skills and intellect to create—a building, for example, or a statue. If we would try to make something exactly like ourselves, we would fail. The product would be different from ourselves, however skillful we are, because it would be something we had only made. On the other hand, we *beget* what is exactly like ourselves because it originates from us. Thus, while a home for me was *made* by my father and mother, and toys were *made* for me as I grew up, only I can be their *begotten* son.

Jesus, the Bible says, is God's "only begotten Son." That does not mean that God reproduced himself as one generation of humans does another. That would imply that the Father once existed without the Son. What it does mean, however, is that the Son, in all eternity, is begotten of the Father. The Son is a perfect image of who the Father is. He exists eternally by the love which the Father has for himself but which he directs toward another like himself. The Son, in turn, adores the Father with all the power of his being.

It is a mystery. How can one God be more than one person at the same time? C. S. Lewis writes:

On the human level one person is one being, and any two persons are two separate beings—just as, in two dimensions one square is one figure, and any two squares are two separate figures. On the Divine level you still find personalities; but up there you find them combined in new ways which we, who do not live on that level, cannot imagine. In God's dimension, so to speak, you find a being who is three persons while remaining one Being, just as a cube is six squares while remaining one cube.[17]

Such love between the Father and the Son is so complete, so energetic, so pure that another person proceeds from it. I say "person" because the Holy Spirit *is* a person. As the love between the Father and Son is personal, so the Spirit, who comes from the Father and Son, is also personal; he is the personal Spirit of God's love.

The Sage talked about an extraordinary marriage which introduced him to the love of God. A good marriage is like God in the sense that the husband and wife love each other. And this love between them creates a spirit in the home, as if it were almost another personality. With God, however, the love has no beginning and end, and the spirit of that love is so real that it is not *like* a person but actually *is* one—the Holy Spirit.

It should not surprise us, therefore, to read in the Bible that the Holy Spirit is the personal embodiment of the love of God (Rom 5:5), nor should it perplex us that the Bible only talks about the love the Father and Son have for each other and not about the love both of them have for the Spirit. The Spirit *is* their love for each other.

Thus the Bible likens the Spirit's presence to a spring of living water. The love of God—that perfect, eternal, pulsating love which God has in himself—is "shed abroad in our hearts" by the presence of the Spirit. Through the Spirit we are enabled not only to behold God but also to exist within him. The Spirit is therefore God's greatest gift. While Jesus brought God down to us in the Incarnation, the Holy Spirit lifts us up into God's very presence and into the dynamic of the relationship he has within himself. We are not the initiators of love; we are not even the direct recipients. Rather, we are the beneficiaries of a love that existed long before we were ever created. The Sage was right. True healing is found not only when we are loved by others but also when we are enlivened by the love others have for one another: the husband for the wife and the wife for the husband, and even more so, the Father for the Son and the Son for the Father. The Holy Spirit introduces us to the rarified atmosphere of the Godhead.

What He Does

The Holy Spirit, then, is the love of God poured into our hearts. Traditional Protestantism teaches that we receive this Spirit at conversion or baptism (Rom 8:9-11; Acts 2:38), or so we are supposed to believe, however remote it is from our experience.

Indeed, it can be and often has been very remote. Many Christians give little indication that they are filled with the Holy Spirit. This is hard to reconcile with the story line of Acts, which emphasizes the regularity of Christians *experiencing* the Spirit and the abnormality of those few "Christians" who showed no sign of being filled with the Spirit (Acts 8, 19). The charismatic movement has exposed this disparity between truth and experience. To solve the problem, it has stressed the need for another experience, called the "baptism of the Holy Spirit," which happens after conversion and is typically confirmed by a visible sign (usually tongues).

The charismatic movement, however, has had its own problems. For example, it has sometimes not known what to do with people who, though vibrant and fruitful Christians, have never had a "second experience." Also, it has tended to teach "techniques" (for instance, how to speak in tongues) in order to manipulate the Spirit to do what supports the movement's own theological presuppositions. That is not altogether honest, and it seems to quench the spontaneous and supernatural work of the Spirit. Moreover, some charismatic theology has relegated the filling of the Spirit to one experience. Hence, once people have been baptized in the Spirit, there is nothing more they can receive. How can that be harmonized with Paul's injunction that we must *keep on being filled* with the Holy Spirit (Eph 5:18)? How can we be filled and yet be filled even fuller?

Consider this analogy. A balloon, whatever its degree of inflation, is *always* filled with air. The difference between a limp balloon and a blown-up balloon is that the latter has *more* air in it. While both are filled up with air, the inflated balloon is fuller because it has been stretched—its capacity for air expanded—so that it can receive more air. Likewise, Jesus has filled us with the Spirit as a deflated balloon is filled with air. But he also *increases our capacity* to receive more of the Spirit until we are "filled with all the fulness of God" (Eph 3:19). The difference between a new Christian and a mature Christian, therefore, is not that the new Christian is only half full but that the mature Christian is more full; the person has been stretched, like a balloon, to take in more of God. It is possible, therefore, to be filled up and yet to become fuller.

How? By asking God, boldly and persistently, so that our capacity to take in his life grows.

And I tell you, Ask, and it will be given you; seek, and you will find; knock, and it will be opened to you. For every one who asks receives, and he who seeks finds, and to him who knocks it will be opened. What father among you, if his son asks for a fish, will instead of a fish give him a serpent; or if he asks for an egg, will give him a scorpion? If you then, who are evil, know how to give good gifts to your children, how much more will the heavenly Father give the Holy Spirit to those who ask him! (Lk 11:9-13)

Once filled with the Spirit and yet seeking to be filled even more, we must begin to explore what the Spirit does, or wants to do. First, the Spirit works *within us* to make us new persons. He confirms our identity as children of God (Rom 8:12-17; Eph 1:12-14). He is the guarantee, or deposit, of what is still coming—our full inheritance. He does this by giving us longings for what is yet to be. He causes us to look ahead, always ahead, toward our homeland, the final place of rest and fullness. Just so does the Holy Spirit awaken us to hope (Ps 42; Rom 8:18-25). While he makes us content, he never lets us be satisfied. He is always whispering in our hearts, "There is more. There is more."

He also leads us into all truth (Jn 16:12-15). He guides us through the maze of biblical truths so that we comprehend *the* truth, which is not merely propositional, not merely moral, but personal. The truth is Christ, and all truths in Scripture point to him. The Spirit thus gives us balance. Like a driver of a bobsled, he protects us from crashing too hard into one wall (the truth of God's sovereignty, for example) or another (human freedom). He keeps guiding us down the run, with all of its twists and turns, until we arrive at the fullness of Christ.

Second, the Holy Spirit also works *among us* to establish a new community. He alters our disposition toward others. He enables us to love all people, especially Christians, however different from us they are. He also takes our bents and basic abilities, charges them with power and directs them toward the service of others. In other words, he captures those things which are natural to us, and by supernatural power refines and shapes them until they become gifts of the Spirit. Natural strengths, so prone to become weaknesses, are empowered and become spiritual strengths for the body of Christ. Ambition and savvy are broken and transformed into sacrifical leadership. Fastidious concern for details gives way to servanthood. Extreme sensitivity to self is replaced by mercy. Judgment is changed into prophecy. Thus the body of Christ thrives under the way the Spirit disciplines and directs its individual members, using what each one has for the rest. The Spirit works among us for the sake of the common good (1 Cor 12).

Finally, the Spirit works *through us* to create a new world. He uses limp actions and timid plans to change society (Acts 1—5). Jesus told his disciples to wait in Jerusalem until the Holy Spirit would come, otherwise their efforts would be only meaningless gestures. They waited, and the Spirit came or, more accurately, exploded. The spoken word pierced the hearts of people; prayers uttered in hope were answered in power; wild dreams were fulfilled. The world was overrun by the gospel. The Spirit thus empowers us for service and prepares the way for our fruitfulness.

How He Works

We are still left with one last question. We understand now *who* the Holy Spirit is and *what* he is supposed to do, but we are still wondering *how* he will do it.

When I was very young my family vacationed once in the Rocky Mountains. I know now that we visited some of the most spectacular sites in the United States (Glacier National Park, Yellowstone, the Tetons) because my parents have since told me all about the trip. Yet in my own mind I can only remember vague impressions of what I saw. I have lingering memories of ominous, cloud-covered peaks and thunderous rivers, and valleys covered with pine forests. Though unclear, these memories are still enough to give me longings for the mountains which I have to this day. They still awaken in me desires to hike through forests and study tall peaks. Images of those mountains are permanently etched into my soul.

The Holy Spirit brands an image of God into our hearts when we become Christians. Thus, when God is present to do some dramatic work in us, that image of him causes us to respond almost instinctively to what God wants to do. The Holy Spirit arouses us to cooperate with the great work God is doing in our lives. He motivates us to be responsive (chapter thirteen). We thus have an internal, almost subconscious sensitivity to God, given to us supernaturally by the indwelling Spirit. The God within us is forever responding to the same God who wants to work on us and through us. The internal presence of God prompts us to yield to the external work of God, to his *initiative* in changing our lives (chapter twelve).

Our experience confirms this truth. What makes us repent of sin, love a wayward brother, dare to believe God for the impossible, sing hymns from the heart or be moved by a sermon is the Holy Spirit responding to whatever God is trying to do in our lives. This explains why it exhausts us to oppose God. When we try to retard what he is doing, we attempt the impossible task of dividing the God within us from the God working on and through us. But God cannot be divided like that. He is one.

The upshot is this: once Christian, we do not have to "make" the Spirit do anything, nor is it necessary to manipulate the Spirit so that we can "get" more of him. We are simply to obey his promptings when he speaks through the Bible, through our friends and enemies or through the reproofs of life. It is as if a wonderful image of the mountains had just flashed into our minds and we raced to see them with inextinguishable joy and awe.

Study Questions
1. The Holy Spirit is a controversial subject these days. What are some of the popular ideas about him in the church?
2. Who is the Holy Spirit to you?
3. What are the different roles the Holy Spirit plays in the Christian life according to John 14:15-17; 16:12-15; Galatians 5:16-24; and 1 Corinthians 12?
4. According to Luke 11:9-13, how do we receive the Holy Spirit?
5. What do you think the Holy Spirit wants to do in you at this point in your life?

Chapter 12

THE GRACE
OF GOD

IT WAS A HOT, HUMID AND lazy Thursday morning, the kind of day you wear as you walk through it. The Sage had come to join my family for breakfast. I had just finished my morning run when I saw him sitting on the porch.

"I was running up the dirt road," I blurted out, "when a bulldozer and pickup passed me. It looked like they were ready to tear something down. Does Edward or Rachel want something taken down?"

"They never mentioned anything to me. Let's go see."

When we arrived, we saw a crew of men surveying an old building that stood about fifty yards south of Edward and Rachel's home. About a year ago they had bought the lot next to theirs; the dilapidated cottage came with it. For years it had been empty, serving only as a haven for the small animal population of the woods. The roof leaked. Many of the windows were broken. The siding was chipped, cracked, bent and rotting. The cottage looked like it belonged in a ghost town. The year before Edward had talked about fixing it up and converting it into a studio. He was never one to move too quickly, however, and so the idea was finally dropped.

"Yeah, this must be it," said one of the crew members. "What a pile of junk. Let's just plow it over and haul it away. I'll call for a heavy truck."

"Wait a minute," the driver of the bulldozer said. "That's a bad idea. There's not enough room here for me to maneuver. I'm afraid I'd take a tree or two down with the house."

"So what's a couple of trees?" the first man said.

"Plenty, when they're not ours. We've been hired to tear down this cottage, not the woods."

"So what do we do?" another of them asked impatiently.

"Let's pull off the siding first. And you, George, can take out the windows. Let's save what we can."

"Save!" George interrupted. "This place just ain't worth savin'. Let's get on with it." Then he marched over to the front porch and took aim with his sledgehammer to knock out one of the porch beams.

"Wait a minute," the driver yelled. "This cottage is worth something. Take a look at those window frames: oak ruined by ugly paint. Check out the chimney: made of smooth riverbed stone. I bet the inside could be beautiful if someone took the time to fix it up. I wish I could get my hands on this place."

"Yeah, and how about this cheap, rotten siding?"

"Added later," he said.

During their entire conversation the Sage and I had been standing about twenty yards away. Suddenly the driver of the bulldozer noticed us and yelled, "Who owns this place? Know why they want it torn down?"

"I don't know," I said as I walked toward them, taking his question as an invitation to join them.

"Where are they right now?" he asked.

"Don't know. They were here last night."

"Perhaps you should wait," the Sage said. "They often go away on Thursdays, but they're usually back by 10:00 A.M. That's only thirty minutes from now."

"We don't have that kind of time," George said. "Let's get goin'." Then he nodded to the other two crew members, who took up hammers and crowbars and went to work on the siding and windows. The driver, who was obviously the man in charge, supervised the work and also carried out the few pieces of furniture left in the house.

About ten minutes later Edward and Rachel drove up. Edward looked surprised.

"What's going on here?" he asked.

"We're tearing down your cottage," the supervisor said. "Oh, by the way, is there anything here you want us to save?"

"What do you mean 'tearing down my cottage'? Whose idea is this?" His voice rose in intensity as shock slowly gave way to anger. "I never asked you to come here!"

Just then another crew member approached.

"What's the problem here?" he said. "I'm the one who got the instructions from our secretary. Some guy—Ed was his name—asked if we could tear down an old building south of his cottage. This must be it. It's old, its south of your house, and your name must be Ed."

Edward exploded.

"My name is Edward, not Ed. I never made such a call. Get off my property or I'll call the police. Rachel! Call the police and tell them vandals are destroying our property."

"Just a minute," George said sharply. "Don't you threaten us like that!"

The two men faced each other squarely. Edward, in spite of his fragile frame, seemed angry enough to swing at a bull, which the man in front of him faintly resembled. I was wondering how I could rescue him in case he did something rash.

"Roger," the supervisor called, "get those instructions out of the pickup. Hurry up."

Roger hesitated. It was hard to tell whether he was taking his time because he was hoping a fight would break out or whether he was feeling uneasy about what the others might learn from the instructions. Perhaps he had committed the unpardonable sin for demolition crews—leading them to the wrong place. He got the instructions and gave them to the supervisor.

"Let's see . . . 8436 S. Shore Drive. Right?" He handed them to Edward.

"Can't you read? This says 5436," Edward said in utter disbelief.

"Impossible," the supervisor said, grabbing the instructions from Edward's hand. But Edward was right. Someone had misread the directions. They had gone to the wrong place.

"You bumbling idiots have just ruined my property! That's a criminal offense. Rachel!" he shouted. "Call a lawyer."

"We're sorry," the supervisor said as he stared coldly at Roger. "It's a mistake anybody could make."

"Mistake! Tell that to my lawyer."

By now the entire crew was standing around Edward. I smelled the scent of violence.

"Wait a minute," Rachel said to Edward, thus relieving some of the tension. "Why can't we hire these men to tear off the old siding and haul all the junk away? Then you and I could spend the rest of the summer renovating it. Maybe you'll get your new studio after all."

"Do you think it can be done?" the Sage asked George.

"I suppose so. Why not? It won't be easy or cheap to renovate, but it's still possible. This place is valuable and it could be beautiful if someone put some time and money into it."

"Well, Edward?" Rachel said superciliously.

"Oh, all right. But what about the building you're supposed to raze?"

"It can wait until tomorrow," George said, eager to appease him.

"Are you sure this is worth it?" Edward asked, still a little angry.

"Positively," George said.

So everyone, including the Sage and me, sprang into action. We had a wonderful time of it, even the crew member who had made the mistake on the address. He was relieved that all was turning out well.

Later that day the Sage and I walked back to our cottage, sore from the hard work and stuffed from the food Rachel had made. We were pleased with what we had accomplished.

Throughout the summer we spent several more days helping Edward and Rachel and so witnessed the gradual transformation of the cabin from a piece of junk to a lovely cottage, all because of a small coincidence and a lot of hard work.

*   *   *

Cleaned Out and Fixed Up

Like that dilapidated cabin, we too are in need of major renovation, as is the church and the whole world. We need to get stripped of our cheap siding, cleaned out and fixed up. We need to be overhauled.

It is a job we cannot do by ourselves. God must take the initiative, or we will forever remain the rubble we are, however much we want to change. Why? Because we are ignorant, stubborn and incapable. We are ignorant, for example, of who we are and of what, by God's grace, we could be. We are oblivious both to our bankruptcy and to our destiny. Ignorance blinds us and distorts our spiritual senses. It makes us satisfied to be far less than what we could be. We want mere gratification; God holds out for our greatness. We want to nibble on garbage; God invites us to a feast. Ignorance dulls us to the spectacular plan God has for our lives.

Stubbornness only complicates the problem. In many cases we simply do not want to change, even if we know we should. We would rather make excuses. We are the way we are because of family, heritage, circumstances or human limitations. It is always someone else's fault. And when we can find no one or nothing to blame, we harden our faces and refuse to budge. "I'm happy just as I am," we say defensively.

Even if we do want to change, we often find it impossible. We are incapable of becoming what we know we could be. Perhaps we try for a while, but then we fall back into the jaws of some habit we want to, but cannot, conquer. Self-hatred haunts us. Lust consumes us. Jealousy tortures us. Laziness catches us in its inescapable web. No matter how sincere our desires, our inability to change exposes the folly of equating Christianity with positive attitudes and ambitious resolutions. Good, hard work is not the essence of Christianity; neither is a sunny attitude toward life. They lead, if anywhere, to false hope; and they create, if anything, false security.

Thomas Merton comments on this:

In getting the best of our secret attachments—ones which we cannot see because they are principles of spiritual blindness—our own initiative is almost always useless. We need to leave the initiative in the hands of God working in our souls either directly in the night of aridity and suffering, or through events and other men. This is where so many holy people break down and go to pieces. As soon as they reach the point where they can no longer see the way and guide themselves by their own light, they refuse to go any further. They have no confidence in anyone except themselves. Their faith is largely an emotional illusion. It is a kind of natural optimism that is stimulated by moral activity and warmed by the approval of other men.[18]

God's Initiative

God must give us grace if we are to grow as disciples. And he does give us grace by taking the initiative to transform us into Christlike creatures. Grace is God's power acting on us to make us what he intends us to be as the Holy Spirit works in our hearts to cause us to respond to his shaping of our lives. Grace, then, is not a static, lifeless concept. Many of us are mistaken to think that grace is more like a cup of warm milk than a cold mountain stream, or more like a cozy womb than loving parents who expect the best from us. God does not accept us as we are so that we can remain that way. God's grace is not merely a tepid, sunny environment. It is a cold shower, a bolt of lightning, a carefully wielded scalpel, a kick in the pants, a passionate embrace—because God wants to make us not nice but new, not decent people but true disciples. He will settle for nothing less.

Imagine that you are an artist, poised to begin work on what you hope will be your greatest sculpture. You have purchased a huge block of marble, and for days now you have been staring at it in your studio. To you it is not a piece of marble; it is a perfect statue held captive in a marble grave. You see in the marble a man and a woman, lovers, embracing as the woman dies in his arms. You want to set them free. So you take up mallet and chisel and strike your first blow. You pound, chip, cut, scrape and sand day after day, removing all the stone that keeps the lovers from living. Finally the image in your mind takes form. Their heads appear. Their eyes live, hers so full of compassion, though she is dying; his so full of pain, though he lives. Their bodies emerge, so passionately, intimately intertwined. His hand gently strokes her beautiful face. Finally you finish and stand back to gaze at this, your final statement to the world. It is perfect.

God, too, is an artist, but the materials for his works of art are not marble or canvas but flesh and blood. We are the ones he wants to shape into beautiful creatures. He, like any artist, sees what ought to be in us and chips away at everything that keeps us from it. That is the essence of God's grace for discipleship, his initiative.

The Use of Circumstance
God takes the initiative to make us Christlike by using our daily experiences and the circumstances of life to transform us. They are his tools. Thus, whether God causes them or allows them, he nevertheless uses circumstances to draw us to him and to make us like him.

Spiritual maturity, therefore, comes not in spite of but by means of our circumstances. What we try to use as excuses for our lack of spiritual progress and as justification for bitterness, immorality, laziness and anxiety, God purposes to use as catalysts for Christian growth. Nothing, as it turns out, can separate us from the love of God. E. Stanley Jones declares, "Don't bear trouble, use it. . . . Take whatever happens—justice and injustice, pleasure and pain, compliment and criticism—take it up into the purpose of your life and make something out of it. Turn it into a testimony. Don't explain evil; exploit it; make it serve you."[19]

This implies that we are always in the *ideal environment* to grow in discipleship. We might not see it; we might not want to admit it; but God's sovereignty insures it. There is simply never a time when he is not shaping our lives by using the stuff of our daily experiences. Suffering works as well as success; pressure as well as prosperity; opposition as well as opportunity. All is used by God to carve the image of Christ into us. We can therefore stop wishing that times were better for us. In one sense they are the best they can be.

David, for example, prepared himself for kingship in various settings and not all of them were pleasant: on the battlefield, fighting Goliath; in the pasture, tending sheep; in caves, fleeing from Saul. The question for David was not whether God was in control (for he knew that he was) but whether David was responsive to God's initiative. And he was, of course. His early years as a shepherd made him content and courageous instead of impatient and cowardly. His years of flight made him loyal and prayerful rather than bitter and selfish. David welcomed the wielding of God's mallet and chisel. He responded to God through his circumstances and so became a great man.

We are required to keep one eye on what is happening *to* us and our other eye on what God is trying to do *in* us. In the past and present are scattered all kinds of circumstances, some chosen and some not, that God wants to use to shape our lives. It may be a person in authority, however kind or cruel; it may be a personal problem or an incident from our past; it may be a defect in our bodies or a flaw in our appearance; it may be a new responsibility, however mundane or exacting; it may be a relationship with a friend or foe.

Open and Discerning

God gives grace by using whatever comes our way to shape our lives. Progress in discipleship, therefore, depends a great deal on our *openness*. If we believe that God is compassionately sovereign, then we can be confident that nothing will be able to obstruct his scheme for our lives. In a sense, he stands invisibly between us and our circumstances, using them as tools for renovation but never allowing them to become instruments of destruction. As the Sage and I discovered on that Thursday morning, God will use even what appears to be coincidence to strip us down and build us up. "If God is for us, who can be against us? [Nothing] will be able to separate us from the love of God" (Rom 8:31, 39 NIV). Underneath the rotten siding of life is pure oak. But we will never know until we let God renovate our lives. The process of stripping down is as necessary as the process of building up. Jesus called it pruning (Jn 15).

The degree of our openness will determine whether we inflate the power of circumstances beyond what they deserve or deflate their power by submitting these circumstances to the reign of God. By God's grace circumstances are the *means* to maturity; by our resistance they are the way to ruin. In either case, they will drive us toward our destiny.

We should be sobered then, by the power of choice we have (as we shall see in chapter thirteen). Daily, hourly, we are saying yes or no to God simply by how we regard the matters closest at hand: our bosses, friends, work assignments, money. Humility welcomes grace; pride shuns it. The late Lord Kenneth Clark, one of England's great art historians, warns us by his regrettable example of how to respond:

> I had a religious experience. It took place in the church of San Lorenzo, but did not seem to be connected with the harmonious beauty of the architecture. I can only say that for a few minutes my whole being was inundated by a kind of heavenly joy, far more intense than anything I had known before. This state of mind lasted for several minutes, and, wonderful though it was,

posed an awkward problem in terms of action. My life was far from blameless: I would have to reform. My family would think I was going mad, and perhaps after all, it was a delusion for I was in every way unworthy of receiving such a flood of grace. Gradually the effect wore off and I made no effort to retain it. I think I was right. I was too deeply embedded in the world to change course. But that I had "felt the finger of God" I am quite sure and, although the memory of this experience has faded, it still helps me to understand the joys of the saints.[20]

Progress in discipleship also requires *discernment* so that we can distinguish between the various *good*s in life and the *best*, available only by God's grace. There is a vast difference between happiness and joy, earthly adulation and spiritual depth, immediate success and true spiritual stature. God promises joy, love and life, until our cup fills and spills over. He is serious about his plan, more serious sometimes than we want him to be. To reach that end, he will even deprive us of momentary pleasure to cultivate in us the character of Christ. That is why Christianity sometimes seems to make life worse for us. At times only a surgeon's scalpel ensures real health. Only by God's initiative can we become mature disciples. Such discernment, however, will keep us from becoming passive and indifferent in the face of evil circumstances. Evil and good are still important concepts for Christians. God is sovereign, but he is not the author of evil, though he uses it for our good. We must acknowledge God's rulership over all of life. But it is imperative that we never regard evil as if its existence did not matter, because it does. Christians should be content, but we should never be satisfied. We must always be vigorously and doggedly opposed to evil, as God is. Paul encouraged slaves to gain their freedom (1 Cor 7:21); but if they failed, he exhorted them to serve their masters as unto the Lord. Daniel did not bend to the capricious will of the king; he was willing, nevertheless, to be thrown to the lions when he resisted the king's command. Opposition, yes; rebellion, no. That's the balance.

Such a balance is impossible to strike unless we acknowledge that God is God. He controls human life, including the ultimate effects of evil. All things serve his purpose. Paul stated this clearly in perhaps the most astonishing verse in the Bible: "God causes all things to work together for good to those who love God, to those who are called according to His purpose" (Rom 8:28 NASB). Peter Kreeft comments on the implications of this verse:

> Every atom in the quadrillion-mile universe and every "chance" event in its trillion-year history is deliberately and perfectly planned and controlled by God for the ultimate end of our good, our heavenly joy. Galaxies revolve and dinosaurs breed and rain falls and people fall in love and uncles smoke cheap cigars and people lose their jobs and we all die—all for our good, the finished product, God's work of art, the kingdom of Heaven. There's nothing outside heaven except hell. Earth is not outside heaven; it is heaven's workshop, heaven's womb.[21]

We can therefore be both responsive to God's grace given to us by means of our circumstances and opposed to the evil inherent in those circumstances. Christians, as Luther said, are both free and enslaved, subject to all things and subject to nothing.

God has the eye to see what individuals, the church and the whole world can become. He is committed to moving us toward that destiny. Though we deserve to be razed and tossed into the junkyard like that beat-up cabin, God nevertheless purposes to renovate us until we are perfectly new and wonderfully complete. For his tools he uses circumstances to accomplish his plan. The initiative is always his. There is evidence of it all around us, if we are discerning enough to look and open enough to respond.

Study Questions

1. What is grace and why do we need it?
2. What do we learn about grace from Ephesians 2:1-10 and 2 Corinthians 12:7-10?
3. When you think of the word *grace*, what comes to mind? How do you think the word is misunderstood?
4. What circumstances in the past has God used to change you?
5. How do you think God is using circumstances to change your life now? In what ways can you be more open and discerning to God's initiatives?

Chapter 13

OUR
RESPONSIVENESS

MOMENTS OF BEAUTY ARE seldom seen unless we have the eyes to see them. The Sage was adept at spotting such moments and generous in pointing them out to me. On one occasion, when we were sitting on the beach, the Sage spotted a simple scene I would have missed. In the distance a father and his son were walking toward us. They seemed to be frozen in a cocoon of mutual delight. To them, nothing else mattered but each other.

The father was sauntering at the edge of the shoreline, just close enough to the water for his feet to be splashed by the bigger waves washing up on the sand. His son, however, was all motion and energy, darting here, jumping there, exploring the little worlds around him. He turned over every piece of driftwood he found. Once it appeared he had discovered a colony of ladybugs living next to a log. He yelled for his dad, and the two of them watched together. The little boy was all questions; the father, all patient answers. Farther down the beach the son found a dead fish. He was fascinated by it. Once again he called for his dad, who immediately walked over and stooped to study it with his son.

Still, the little boy had too much energy to stay motionless. This time he ventured into the water, cautiously at first, then more boldly. Twice he looked back at his father, who was watching him warily. He warned him not to go out too far, but his son ignored his advice. This was too much fun for caution!

Suddenly a big wave crashed near the shore and knocked him over, causing him to disappear momentarily under the water. He was so frightened that when his head reappeared he screamed even before he had time to breath. He had not expected waves to be so powerful! His dad, however, had jumped to action long before his son cried out. The moment he saw the wave coming he raced toward the boy. He grabbed him gently, gave him a hug and then hoisted him up on his shoulders, far above the threatening water.

Soon his son was emboldened again. He indicated that he wanted to get down and his father complied. This time he ran far ahead, perhaps a hundred yards. He probably would have gone even farther had he not seen a Labrador retriever bounding toward him. He took one look, turned on his heels and sprinted toward his dad as if he had just seen a monster. Fear drove him.

The whole scene was rather comical. The dog ran much faster than the boy, of course, but he was also much farther away. So a race was on. Would the dog reach the boy before the boy reached his father?

Probably not. But the father eliminated the risk by jogging toward his son, whom he swept up into his arms just before the dog skidded to a halt at his feet. That little boy climbed all the way to the top of his father before he dared to look at this ferocious creature. The father laughed.

As it turned out, the dog was friendly. So the father began, very slowly, to introduce his son and the dog to each other. His son, still afraid, was far more cautious than the dog, whose wagging tail and eager bark demonstrated his exuberance. Soon he was sitting on his dad's lap, petting the dog's head. Not long after that the two of them were scampering away together.

*   *   *

Biblical Responsiveness

The Christian faith pries our closed universe open. It gives life a dimension that transcends and yet animates our earthly life. It shines light and imparts freshness into the dark, stuffy and dusty world in which we live. The Lord God reigns, and he sent Jesus to prove it. That shows how open the universe is! It ought to make life different for us, not merely tolerable but spectacular, engaging and adventurous.

God invaded this world to announce and make possible what he has in mind for us. He wants to transform us, the church and the entire world. To do that he promises to give us power that works within us and upon us. By using the stuff of daily experience as a builder uses tools to renovate an old building, he transforms us.

God only requires us to be *responsive.* That is the one choice we must make. Responsiveness is unconditional openness to God's grace within the circumstances in which we live. It is our way of acknowledging that God, being both sovereign and good, has designed a wonderful destiny for us. It is our way of affirming that the real crucible of life for us is the place where God's power confronts our circumstances and uses them for an ultimate good. Responsiveness makes Christianity more than a set of doctrines; it makes it a dynamic, livable faith, always energetic, always relevant, always applicable—and sometimes very tough.

Luke's story about Jesus' adolescent visit to the Temple shows us how Jesus was responsive to God. It was during the Passover, when pilgrims from all over Palestine traveled in large groups to Jerusalem to celebrate and worship. Jesus' parents let him accompany them. On their journey back to Nazareth, however, they discovered that he was absent from the company, and so they returned quickly to Jerusalem to search for him. Luke does not tell us what they were thinking. We can surmise, however, that as time elapsed they began to imagine the worst: Jesus had been captured and sold into slavery, he had been beaten and left to die in some back alley, or he was lost and afraid. For three long days they looked frantically for him. Finally, exhausted and despairing, they wandered into the Temple to ask God for help and guidance.

Instead, they found Jesus. He was sitting among the teachers, questioning them and impressing them with his wisdom.

"Why have you treated us so?" his mother asked anxiously.

"Didn't you know that I am supposed to be in my Father's house?" Jesus replied incredulously. Luke says that his parents did not understand. Rather, they insisted that he return with them to Nazareth.

At that moment Jesus could have used their ignorance to excuse disobedience. After all, they were wrong. Nevertheless, Jesus was submissive to them. He went back to Nazareth, where he was largely isolated from the mainstream of Israel's religious life and there he stayed for eighteen more years. Luke makes the lesson clear in his final remark: "And Jesus increased in wisdom and in stature, and in favor with God and man" (Lk 2:52). His unconditional openness to God, demonstrated by his obedience to his parents, moved him toward maturity.

The apostle Paul used the word *submission* to teach the same principle. He commanded slaves to be submissive to their masters, wives to their husbands, children to their parents, "as unto the Lord" (Eph 5:21—6:9). He encouraged them to acknowledge the sovereignty of God which overruled the negative consequences of occupying their subordinate stations in life. Masters, husbands and parents were also enjoined to be submissive, although in different ways, by humbly and graciously fulfilling their responsibilities as if the Lord were *their* earthly master. Again, Paul charged them to be responsive to God, considering their circumstances.

There are countless examples of responsiveness in the Bible. Joseph was responsive to God even when he was thrown into prison. Moses was responsive to God during the years he spent in the wilderness. Ruth was responsive to God after she lost her Jewish husband. Mary was submissive to God after the angel announced the news of her miraculous pregnancy. "Let it be to me according to your word," she said to the angel. These and many others were responsive to God in the tough circumstances they faced. They knew that God was bigger, and they knew that God had bigger plans in mind for them.

The point is that not even our wildest dreams could fathom the incredible destiny awaiting us, both now and in the age to come. Jesus said to Peter, "What I am doing you do not know now, but afterward you will understand." With Peter, we must believe God for the impossible and remain unconditionally open to him as he wields his tools to break us of sin and shape us into new creatures. Our circumstances are the very tools he often finds most useful. Responsiveness welcomes God's initiative and affirms that God is in control.

Practical Requirements

Responsiveness has certain practical requirements: faith, knowledge, humility, endurance. Faith is a way of *seeing* both a person—God—and a process—transformation. Faith has no power in itself; it gets its value from the object that inspires it. When the disciples asked Jesus how they could get more faith, he told them that a mustard seed of faith was enough (Lk 17:5-6). More or less is not the point. What matters is whom or what the faith is in. God must be both the source and goal of our faith, and his plan for our lives must be what awakens faith and fortifies us against the tyranny of the present (Heb 11:1).

Faith is always tested. Sarah, for example, had to wait for a child. She finally grew so old that she was no longer able to have children unless God intervened. God did, and Isaac was born. David had to wait for a throne. He learned that the wilderness was a long way from the palace. Jesus had to wait for his exaltation. The darkness of the cross tempted him, no doubt, to wonder about God's promise. We, too, must wait for God to finish his work in us. Faith is sometimes hard to sustain when it is challenged by situations that appear to run contrary to God's design. Sometimes the evidence in support of God's goodness seems meager. Failure at work tests our confidence in God's ability to provide. Conflicts among family members cause us to wonder whether God wants to give us peace. These times of testing lead us into the dark night of the soul, where we meet God. Sometimes we come to know God and learn to love God when we have only God and nothing else.

Tested faith becomes bold faith. In time we will find ourselves not only believing *in* God but also believing God *for* some great work he wants us to accomplish. I have often been amazed by the confidence of the great figures of the Bible. How, I have asked, did they know so clearly what God wanted them to accomplish? How did Nehemiah know God wanted him to rebuild the wall of Jerusalem? How did Peter know God wanted him to heal that lame man? Their faith was reckless, almost brazen, yet never presumptuous or capricious. By faith they simply knew. And by faith we will know what it is God wants to do in and through us. Bold faith will give us a vision of what will someday be because of our work.

Second, faith must be accompanied by *knowledge;* but it must be a particular kind of knowledge. Mere information is not enough. We gain real knowledge when biblical truth merges with human experience; only that kind of knowledge makes us wise. It is applicable in the immediate and livable for a lifetime. To acquire it, we must be rigorous students of the Bible, for faith must be illumined by God's ways. But we must also be students of life, for faith must be embedded in reality. So if we are living under pressure, we should study the life of David. If leaders, we ought to read about Nehemiah. If timid, we should examine 1 Timothy. If members of a lifeless, fragmented church, we should explore 1 Corinthians. It is not enough merely to want to be responsive to God. We must also know *how.* The knowledge of Scripture will tell us.

Third, *humility* makes knowledge useful because it makes us unconditionally teachable. All people, of course, are teachable some of the time. The most arrogant athlete is willing to learn from a famous coach; an intellectual snob will study under a great scholar. Pride, however, keeps us from true teachableness. Pride sets up categories—"superior" and "inferior"—that prevent us from learning from the little people who are often the most able to enlarge our worlds. Pride causes us to reserve the right to decide when, where, how and from whom we will learn. That leads not to wisdom but to arrogance, and ultimately to ignorance (see chapter fourteen).

Humility sets no boundaries. It gives God the freedom to teach us whenever, wherever and however he wishes. Sometimes janitors have a few things to say to scholars, grandmothers to children, teen-agers to their parents, sinners to saints, donkeys to the Balaams in this world. Humility embraces knowledge, whatever the source is; its goal is not superiority but conformity to Christ.

Finally, *endurance* protects us from being slaves to the immediate. Endurance keeps us from establishing time limits for God. We are willing to wait for the full effect of what God wants to do in us. If God purposes to make us diamonds, endurance keeps us from backing out when we feel like coal. We are willing to take the pressure, however great it is, however long it lasts, until God has finished his work (Heb 12:1-3).

No Regrets

Responsiveness to God's initiative frees us from bondage to the past. It allows us to live with no regrets. However bad, the past no longer has to smother our enthusiasm and stifle our progress. Responsiveness gives God the chance to use even the worst in the past to benefit us in the future.

We need this kind of freedom and hope. There are many of us who believe that God offers us forgiveness for past sins but that, however great the forgiveness, we still have to live with the *regret* of the past. And there is nothing we can do about it. Regret makes us want to erase parts of our past and start all over. It leads to wishful thinking: "If only I could have that Saturday night back";

"If only I could get back my first year of marriage and start all over"; "If only I had not chosen that set of friends"; "If only I could have my daughter back again"; "If only I hadn't been so pushy in my job."

Regret is often aggravated by the consequences of past decisions that still haunt us. These make it all the more bitter. Some of us, in other words, are still staring at pasts that refuse to die: rebellious children, debt from unwise business ventures, boring jobs, unhappy marriages. It tempts us to doubt God's goodness. If God has forgiven us, we think, then why do we suffer from such horrible consequences? Why such nagging regret?

True responsiveness forces us to face the past and not run from it. Eventually we find hope, healing and triumph. We can believe that God will give us power: to endure, to make our apologies, to rebuild our marriages, to pay off our debts, to kick our bad habits, to establish new convictions. We can also believe that God is so great that he will bless us through the very consequences we face.

"We know that in *everything* God works for good with those who love him, who are called according to his purpose" (Rom 8:28). God is able to turn losses into gains. He is so committed to us that in spite of our sin he not only forgives but also redeems. He not only saves us from the misery of our past but also blesses us through it. No sin—adultery with a next-door neighbor, abuse of a marriage partner, burning jealousy of a wealthy friend, slanderous remarks about a colleague, drunkenness at a party or participation in a corrupt business—can separate us from the love of God once we repent. Oscar Wilde once said, "No man is rich enough to buy back his past." But we can say to Wilde, "Yes, but God is gracious enough to redeem it." Grace is found, then, in the very past from which we are tempted to run. Responsiveness leads to no regrets (2 Cor 7:5-12).

Free to Be Weak and Detached
Responsiveness lets us be weak. It liberates us from trying to prove our own spiritual adequacy. We do not always need a hospitable

environment in which to grow as disciples, nor do we have to be in control. We do not have to rely on our natural strengths. In fact, we can try our hands at tasks in which we are sure to fail. We can dare to do new things, however great the risk. We can face opposition without fleeing or fighting defensively. "I will all the more gladly boast of my weaknesses, that the power of Christ may rest upon me. For the sake of Christ, then, I am content with weaknesses, insults, hardships, persecutions, and calamities; for when I am weak, then I am strong" (2 Cor 12:9-10).

But responsiveness also frees us from living for the self. We are not dependent on circumstances for our happiness and promotions for our security. Thus we are able to approach the world and even change the world in total freedom, never doing anything for ourselves but always for a greater good. We can maintain a detachment from the world's prizes and pleasures so that they are not treated as ultimates. Responsiveness gives us the stature we need to transform the world for Christ and not for ourselves, to make Christ victor over the world rather than the world victor over us, to inhabit the world with a spirit which undermines its own. History is packed with examples of people whose efforts to change the world were corrupted by the very persons and institutions they wanted to change. They were motivated to serve self above God. Responsiveness keeps us pure because God remains our focal point. It makes our vision of a better world true to the kingdom of God and not to selfish ambition.

The Sage and I spotted a father and son walking on the beach. The boy was growing in stature because he was responsive to his father, who was acting as a buffer between his son and the threatening world around him. That is how God wants us to respond to him, one hand reaching up to him, the other reaching out to the world. For if we want to be as loving and strong as that father, then we must learn to be as trusting and responsive as his son.

Study Questions
1. What does it mean to be responsive to a spouse? a sibling? an employer?

God?

2. Responsiveness is unconditional openness to God, considering our circumstances. What can we learn about responsiveness from King Jehoshaphat in 2 Chronicles 20?

3. How do the following enable us to be responsive: faith in God, knowledge, humility and endurance?

4. What are the circumstances you are facing right now? How can you be responsive to God through them?

V
KNOWING
THE
ENEMY

Discipleship gets more complicated and costly when we consider the obstacles we face. We need power not only to overcome our weakness and inadequacy but also to battle two forces that resist our growing in intimacy with God and making progress toward Christlikeness. Pride makes us hostile toward God's sovereignty. It strips the universe of its ultimate authority and then makes us feel superior to everyone else. Pride leads to terrible self-deception and makes us vulnerable to demonic influence (chapter fourteen). Further, evil distorts the good universe God has made and perverts God's truth. At its heart evil is personal, an expression of the heart of man. But more, it is also a personality, Satan, who is rebellious against God and determined to undermine God's scheme for history. He is the deceiver, the tempter, the accuser (chapter fifteen). To explore the problem of pride, then, we return to the Sage. Gossip about him explains one of the chief characteristics of pride.

Chapter 14

PRIDE, THE
QUIET MASTER

To THE LOCAL TOWNSPEOPLE many of the summer vacation-
ers were something of a novelty, since most of them lived well
outside the acceptable boundaries of normality. Their peculiarities—or I should say *our* peculiarities, since I was numbered among
them—were one of the favorite topics of conversation in town.

No one drew more gossip than the Sage. I'm not sure why.
Perhaps they were fascinated by his unknown past or his many
interests. In any case, he was constantly being scrutinized and
analyzed. Once, when a young female friend came to visit him (the
daughter of the janitor, if you remember), the talk in town raged
out of control for over a week. By the time my mother heard about
it at the hairdresser (the barbershop was just as bad), the report
was that the Sage was entertaining young, sensuous women at

least once a week. Some said that he had a strange, mystical power over people, as if he were a spider with an uncanny ability to draw them into his web. I even heard that my parents and I, too, had fallen under his spell. I suppose they were right, if friendship could be considered a spell. But unlike me, the Sage mostly ignored it. I suspected that he had been talked about before and was used to it.

Only once was the gossip confronted directly. My dad, the Sage and I had driven into town for coffee. We did this about four or five times during the summer, always on Saturday mornings. The restaurant we went to was a popular meeting place for the locals. The layout was quite open, so that many people could participate in the same conversation. Only the booths, which had very high backs, kept at least part of the restaurant private.

We arrived at 7:00 A.M., before the rush, and seated ourselves at the most secluded booth in the back of the restaurant. My dad and the Sage ordered coffee and rolls; I ordered breakfast. Then we settled into a conversation about fishing, one of Dad's favorite topics. Naturally, Dad and the Sage started to swap old fishing stories. Soon (out of boredom) my attention was diverted, first by the arrival of my breakfast and then by the presence of the townspeople. I noticed that a few of the old-timers were seated up front at a couple of tables. Three families had also just entered the café. Finally, two gentlemen were seated at the booth next to ours. Neither had taken any notice of me, even though I was eyeing their every move. One of them, as I remember, was the town grocer. The other I had never seen before. They were absorbed in their discussion. They talked just loud enough for me to hear.

"Say," one of them said, "I heard that the old man is wanted by the law back in New York. Tax evasion, I think."

"Is that right! How'd you hear that?"

"Ed Braffit told me just yesterday. Said that the old man came out here to escape the law. Braffit told me he owes over $5,000."

"Anybody gonna turn him in?"

"Don't know. The sheriff knows, too, but I haven't heard if he plans to do anything. Do you think something oughta be done?"

"Suppose so. But who, how, where—that's another matter. Thing's a little delicate, you know."

I recognized immediately whom they were talking about. I was rather amused since I knew that the Sage had been audited the year before. The government had discovered that they owed *him* money.

"I also heard he's a pacifist," the first man said. "Can you believe it?"

"Hardly. A man of his age, living through WW 2, a pacifist? A disgrace to our country! Sounds like a New Yorker. Lot of them are weird out there."

"Well, he couldn't have seen what I saw during the war or he'd be no pacifist. Them Japs were cruel, stubborn, cold-blooded. It took the bomb to make 'em surrender."

"I guess you can't expect much from a man who's been divorced four times. Heard his last wife cracked up."

"Can't hold no job neither. I bet he's not even a lawyer. All rumor, my guess is. I sure wouldn't want him representing me."

"In fact, I heard . . ."

Just then my concentration was interrupted by my dad. "Let's go, son," he said to me.

"Maybe we can still get a little fishing in," the Sage added.

So they stood up. Suddenly I realized that I was about to see something extraordinary. I quickly slid out of the booth and stood where I could see this little drama unfold. The two men saw me and smiled politely. One of them even said, "Howdy, young man," before returning to his private discussion with the man across the table.

Then the Sage turned around, looked directly at them and said, "A pleasant day, don't you think? Enjoying your coffee and conversation?"

Though I am sure he had not heard a word of what they had said, it *appeared* as if he had heard everything and was meeting their gossip head-on. Their faces almost fell off. They stared at the Sage, too dumbfounded to be embarrassed, too surprised to say a word.

The Sage waited for some kind of reply. When he got none, he said, as if following a script, "You must have been discussing a very important topic. Please continue, gentlemen. I only wish I could join you." Then he smiled and walked away.

They had been found out, or so they thought. They were standing naked in the café; the Sage was holding their clothes; I was taking their picture. It was wonderful.

At the cashier's counter I asked my dad if I could go back to leave the tip. I had one last thing I wanted to do. When I walked toward them (they were still looking at me, glassy-eyed), I gave them an icy stare to erase any doubts in their minds. Yes, we had heard *every word they had said.*

"What makes you so happy today?" my dad asked me on the drive back to the cottage.

"Oh, nothing. I'm just thinking of all the humorous stories about the Sage circulating in town."

"Jealousy," my dad said. "Here'a a man who's accomplished something. He's independent, well educated, from out East. That bothers people."

"I'm not so sure about that," the Sage said. "Still, I've observed one thing: people tend to think in comparatives. What they want is to be better than everybody else."

"Competition?" I said.

"Yes, competition," the Sage replied. "And there are lots of ways to compete. Some are less obvious than others."

"Gossip?" I asked.

"Even gossip. That's a deadly kind of competition," the Sage said.

"So's fishing," my dad said, laughing. "And I shall prove myself the superior to both of you."

That day, thank goodness, Dad didn't catch a thing.

*   *   *

The Invisible Monster
Pride subverts discipleship. Set next to it, all our other sins—past,

present and future—pale in comparison. Pride seizes the divine image stamped in us, withdraws it from God's protection and rule and flaunts it in God's face. It makes us monsters. Like modern technology, whose advances have sent us into space but also produced the nuclear bomb, human life has a capacity for greatness, but has deteriorated under the tyranny of pride into abject decadence and misery. Pogroms, wars, oppression and materialism have been the lot of humanity and will continue to be.

Pride exalts the self. Essentially it is self-preoccupation. Yet it is hard to spot and even harder to overcome. Rarely does a person admit to having the vice we call *pride*, although it is the one quality we identify most readily in others. We might say that we are lazy, cowardly, arrogant, stubborn, self-pitying, even rotten, or we may say we are proud of our accomplishments or our person, but we never list pride as one of our shortcomings. Pride hides itself well. It is the silent and invisible master of the house. It wields power without ever being noticed.

We can observe two particularly popular camouflages for pride. First, pride hides itself behind low self-esteem, which is considered by many to be the most universal and serious problem in Western society. The word *problem* is used intentionally. As long as we have the *problem* of low self-esteem, we usually assume that we are free from the *sin* of pride. How could we despise ourselves and be proud at the same time?

Quite easily, as it turns out. The two are not mutually exclusive, just as poverty and materialism are not. We can be both proud and self-rejecting. Low self-esteem is, of course, a legitimate problem. Many of us have been the butt of cruel jokes, the victim of parental or peer rejection, the target of sneers and abuse, a party to failure. We have received many blows to our sensitive egos, causing agony and pain.

Low self-esteem, however, is not our only problem, nor is it our biggest problem. Pride is. Self-preoccupation can surface as self-hatred just as easily as self-love. We use our lack of self-appreciation to excuse depression, moodiness, irresponsibility, ingratitude, lack of love, busyness and envy. Low self-esteem does not exclude pride. It only prevents our seeing it.

Jesus assumed we have self-love. "Love your neighbor as yourself" (Mt 22:39), he said. This has often been interpreted as a command for us to love ourselves; but Jesus had the opposite in mind. Our problem is not a lack of concern for self, it is a failure to show as much concern for others as we have for ourselves. Most of us are not guilty of too little attention to self; we are guilty of too much. We have little love left over for anyone else. Yet we persist in asking, "How can we love others if we don't love ourselves first?"

Paradoxically, we gain self-esteem when we die to self-preoccupation, submit ourselves to the mastery of Christ and lose ourselves in the love of God and in serving the needs of others. Humility, not pride, is the proper companion to healthy self-love, because humility draws attention to who God is and what we can become by his grace.

Second, pride conceals itself behind emotional and even physical sickness. Deviance, disorder, depression, despair, neurosis—these are ideal covers for pride. Not that they are insignificant problems. Such sicknesses are serious and they plague many people. Still, they do not eliminate pride. They only make it harder to spot.

We can see why. To overcome pride God demands repentance of us, which is an act of the will and implies that we are responsible for who we are and what we do. Psychological sickness, on the other hand, requires treatment. It is not *our* fault that we are sick. It is fate, an unfortunate roll of the dice, bad luck, unloving parents, circumstances. It is hardly something for which we can take responsibility. No one would choose to live that way. Chance, not choice, rules.

In *The Abolition of Man* C. S. Lewis argues that once people no longer answer for their actions, they cease to be human. Instead, they are merely the product of forces acting on them, a collage of impulses, drives, feelings, complexes and desires that dominate them and determine their behavior. If people are sick, then they are no longer sinful. They need diagnosis and treatment, not discipline. The opinions of the experts, who must determine the nature and extent of the sickness and the kind of treatment it requires, hold sway. While such expertise is often helpful, it is dangerous when it deprives people of the right—and need, as it turns out—to take responsibility for their actions.

Further, sickness often implicates others. We become the "victim" of their wrongs. If we have a problem, it is their fault; if there is going to be a solution, it must be their doing. We are, in other words, at the mercy of others—the beneficiaries of their goodness, the victims of their cruelty.

Imagine a world in which everyone is a victim. It would boil with hate, bitterness, greed, jealousy, anger, violence; yet no one is responsible. Everyone's sin is not only the result of sickness but also the product of someone else's sin, which in turn is caused by sickness. All are victims; none are offenders. We are closer to that world than we think.

When God Is Not God
To purge ourselves of pride, we must first know what it really is. Pride is the one sin that directly challenges God. It resists and denies his radical loyalty to us and his plan for our lives. Pride is our *refusal to acknowledge that God is God,* that he rightfully occupies the center of life and that he therefore deserves our worship and obedience. That God *is* at the center of the universe is obvious to all, for God created us with the capacity to know him. There is evidence of his existence and power everywhere. We have chosen, says Paul, to suppress this truth and exalt the created above the creator. We have become idolators (Rom 1:19-21).

Pride exalts the self above God. It lures us into seeking independence from him and deludes us in thinking we can be equal to him. Pride challenges God's right to be at the center of life. The Hebrews called such independence "the knowledge of good and evil." Older children want and should have independence from their parents. But it is something we should never seek from God because we can never outgrow our dependence on him.

Pride has often been compared to rebellion or anarchy. A child's rebellion against his parents exceeds the gravity of mere disobedience. Rebellion challenges the right of parents to *be* parents. How can parents discipline such rebellion when their very exercise of discipline, representing one of the responsibilities of parenthood, is spurned? Likewise, the evil of anarchy surpasses mere civil wrongdoing; it challenges the right of the state to function as the state. Anarchists refuse to acknowledge that the state even exists. Eventually the authority of the state clashes with the philosophy of the anarchist. Order and chaos cannot exist at the same time. Neither can God and pride. They are mutually exclusive.

Pride causes us to defy God and everything important to him. It wants chaos, and that is what it gets. But a world without God is a world falling apart. To depose God and succeed is impossible. His robes are too weighty for us to wear, his throne too big, his dominion too great. We cannot take his place. Attempts to supersede him lead to incredible anxiety, insecurity, fear and failure. Life itself ceases to make sense. It loses its symmetry and balance. Rules are changed to fit our liking.

Pride always bears offspring; although different in appearance, they are all monsters.[22] Because we want to view ourselves as equal to God, we become envious of people who have more wealth, have greater ability or possess greater virtue than we do, because these point to our shortcomings. Envy does not inspire us to higher achievement but causes us to diminish the success of others until a bland, base equality rules in culture.

Because we see ourselves as the center of the universe, we become embittered when wants, which are viewed as rights, go unfulfilled. We begin to think that we deserve more than we have and get angry when deprived of it by people or circumstances. Further, life's difficulties and challenges cause us to be dejected, fainthearted, preoccupied with triviality, sluggish, desireless. We become slothful, unwilling to set our sights on the higher callings of life, however exacting the standards. We develop a hatred of anything that entails effort, a repugnance of what requires us to forgo immediate pleasure for future achievement.

Pride also makes us greedy, obsessed not so much with possessions as with the idea of possessing, which supposedly proves our powerfulness. Our avarice makes us crave for more just for the sake of having more. This obsession with having and possessing causes us to be gluttons, addicted to whatever we think brings us pleasure, whether it be food or health or diets or drugs or alcohol. Ultimately gluttony is rooted in boredom. We lose the capacity to dream of what could be, should we gain the will to work and the confidence to believe in the grace of God. Finally, we lust. The sensual replaces the spiritual. We reduce life to the pleasure we can gain. God's standards for beauty, truth and love are jettisoned for base gratification.

I'm O.K., You're Not

Pride makes constant comparisons. By refusing to acknowledge that God is God, we suddenly find ourselves living in a world that lacks a central reference point. A huge vacuum of authority and perspective engulfs us. How can we find our places? When we stop looking up, we start looking around or down. We usually see our neighbors first.

They become our competitors. Since we all want to be at the center of things—a position only God can occupy—we must all fight against each other to get it. So we start to think in terms of "better" and "worse." We become obsessed with the accomplishments and popularity of others. We find it very difficult to take pleasure in the successes of others; we believe that success is such a rare commodity that we cannot be happy when one person accumulates too much of it.

Some of this competition is organized—in education, sports and the marketplace—and is usually harmless and perhaps even helpful, challenging us to do our best and to innovate. Most of it, however, is more insidious. Fads and styles launch us into the jetstream of popular culture. Whoever wears the latest fashions is "better" than those who cannot afford to. Gossip puts others down so that we can rise up. As we saw in the opening sketch, the only way some of the townspeople could prove their superiority was by running down the Sage. Racial prejudice is a classic example of how desperate we can be to prove our superiority over others. Membership in a denomination, a club or an organization often serves the same end. We gain certain distinctives, whether they be doctrinal, socioeconomic, racial or cultural, that make us feel we are better than others.

This explains why, for most of us, enough is never really enough, not until we have *more* than everyone else. We are forever calculating our relative place in the social order. If we spot people still "above" us, though there might be more people "below" us, we cannot let ourselves rest. While there are many reasons for our desire to excel, accumulate wealth and advance ourselves, one of them is our competitive nature. C. S. Lewis observed:

> I pointed out a moment ago that the more pride one had, the more one disliked pride in others. In fact, if you want to find out how proud you are the easiest way is to ask yourself, "How much do I dislike it when other people snub me, or refuse to take any notice of me, or shove their oar in, or patronise me, or refuse me, or show off?" The point is that each person's pride is in competition with everyone else's pride. It is because I wanted to be the big noise at the party that I am so annoyed at someone else being the big noise. Two of a trade never agree. Now what you want to get clear is that Pride is *essentially* competitive—is competitive by its very nature—while other vices are competitive only, so to speak, by accident. Pride gets no pleasure out of having something, only out of having more of it than the next man.[23]

Because it is competitive, pride divides us from others and deprives us of our humanity. Pride makes us exalt our distinctives—that we are communists or capitalists, athletes or musicians, educated or pragmatic—and thus ignore the common roots of our fragile and yet noble condition. Just recently I attended the funeral of a friend's mother who died suddenly of a brain hemorrhage. As we mourned together, the family and friends, I felt we had a solidarity with the entire human race at that moment because we were aware of our mortality. Life was reduced to the simple, the tenuous, the basic. It did not matter what we looked like or what we were good at. Her death united us in our desire to survive with a little dignity and hope. Such a stark, common experience penetrates skin color, ideologies, successes, and forces us to the very foundation of life. We are made to be sensitive to the cry of a baby, the frailty of our bodies, the horror of death, the needs of humanity, the plight of suffering. Such experiences make us human, something from which pride recoils. How easily we forget that the people we are trying to beat were born like us, will die like us and are one with us.

Pride and Self-Deception
Pride deceives the self. Since few of us consistently win and yet all of us are proud, there must be a way in which pride can continue to thrive. And so there is. We delude ourselves into thinking we are better than we are, in spite of the hard evidence of our failure or mediocrity indicating otherwise.

Honesty with ourselves would show how average most of us are. Pride therefore must avoid the truth—for good reason. Full self-knowledge causes despair unless knowledge of God precedes it. None of us will dare to see our true selves unless we allow the mercy of God to embrace us first. "Apart from me you can do nothing." Thus, if we reject God, we must reject knowledge of ourselves, too. We have no choice; we simply must pretend. Adam and Eve dressed in fig leaves to cover their nakedness, the symbol of their frailty, because they could not tolerate seeing the infinite chasm between their real condition and their aspired status. Neither can we.

Observe your friends at a social function sometime. You will notice that most people there, including yourself, are trying to impress the people around them. Our methods may vary, but the result is the same: self-deception. As long as we are away from God, we cannot feel at home with ourselves. We cannot be the lovers, the thinkers, the artists, the students, the homemakers and the friends God wants us to be. As we observed in chapter seven, in pretending to be what we are not, we lose sight of what we could be. We sacrifice our true character by conforming to the popular definitions of "unique" and "independent." Self-deception makes us just like everybody else. What irony! We labor so hard to be unusual and end up being poor imitations of a cultural norm. Merton points out this distinction between personal identity and cultural conformity:

> The person must be rescued from the individual. The free son of God must be saved from the conformist slave of fantasy, passion and convention. The creative and mysterious inner self must be delivered from the wasteful, hedonistic and destructive ego that seeks only to cover itself with disguises. Every movement of my own natural appetite, even though my nature is good in itself, tends in one way or another to keep alive in me the illusion that is opposed to God's reality living within me. Even though my natural acts are good they have a tendency, when they are only natural, to concentrate my faculties on the man that I am not, the one I cannot be, the false self in me, the character that God does not know.[24]

Dying to Pride

Can we overcome pride? The first and most important step toward ridding ourselves of pride is to admit we have it. All excuses and euphemisms must die. We must be willing to say, "Yes, I am proud." On a "60 Minutes" program Mike Wallace interviewed Yehiel Dinur, a survivor of the Nazi concentration camps and, in 1961, a witness against Adolf Eichmann at his trial in Israel. A film clip from that trial showed Dinur walking into the courtroom. When he saw Eichmann he broke down and wept, finally collapsing on the floor. As Wallace discovered in the interview, Dinur was not at that moment filled with hatred and bitterness. His emotions swelled and finally burst because he saw for the first time that Eichmann was an ordinary human being. He told Wallace, "I was afraid about myself. . . . I saw that I am capable to do this. I am exactly like him."

We, too, should be afraid of ourselves. A sober view of pride is necessary if we want to grow in our discipleship, and an awareness of our capacity for evil will do much to make us appreciate the work of Jesus Christ. Only he can set us free; only he can save us from ourselves. Only he can prod us toward our greater destiny, Christ-likeness.

Study Questions
1. Pride is not a popular topic these days. Either it is considered a virtue, or it is camouflaged by other, more "serious" problems. Can you think of some examples of the former? the latter?
2. What do we learn about pride in Genesis 3:1-7?
3. What do we learn about the consequences of pride in Romans 1:18-32? John 8:39-47?
4. Have you ever deceived yourself in the past? How? Do you remember ever having had pride exposed in your life? How?
5. Do you know of any pride in your life right now? Are there circumstances in your life in which you refuse to acknowledge that God is the center of life? Are there people with whom you are comparing yourself and against whom you are competing? Are you deceiving yourself about who you are?
6. Read 1 John 1:5-9.

Chapter 15

EVIL AND THE
PERSONALITY
BEHIND IT

DURING JULY I HEARD NEWS of a party some of my friends had
organized in Grand Rapids. They had wanted to keep it small,
twenty-five people or so, and they had intended to allow only beer.
But the word got out and, by the time it was all over, a hundred
twenty-five people had dropped in, many of whom brought liquor
and drugs. The police crashed it and arrested a few of them, including one of my closer friends. Worse yet, a sixteen-year-old girl
drowned during a midnight swim. Her friends thought her
screams were fake, and so they ignored her until it was too late.
I didn't know her. Just the same, I couldn't shake the story from
my mind. In my imagination I saw her sinking under the waves and

heard her screaming for help.

"It seems so hard to put your finger on," I said to the Sage. "I mean, nobody's at fault, and yet everybody is. I want to blame my friends and to feel sorry for them at the same time."

"Evil forces us into that kind of dilemma," he said. "that should tell us something, I think. Evil comes from people. And yet it can be bigger than people too. I believe that pure evil has invaded our planet from the outside and exploited the opening it found in the human heart."

"How?" I asked.

"Let me tell you a story. About three hundred years ago one of the phases of the Black Death swept through England. In the summer of 1665 it raged through London. Nearly twenty per cent of the city's population died. Over half of the survivors fled for safety, carrying the disease with them and so spreading it over the countryside. In September of that same year the small town of Eyam also fell victim, but only about seventy-five people died before the disease was arrested.

"The plague drove people to superstition and cruelty. You know the nursery rhyme, 'Ring-a Ring of roses, A pocketful of posies, Atishou! Atishou! We all fall down!' It originated at that time. It referred to the rosy mark on the chest of plague victims, the nosegays that people carried hoping to prevent infection and the convulsive sneezing that turned out to be a prelude to death. There were hysterical flare-ups of anti-Semitism, incidences of religious fanaticism and examples of irrational selfishness. You see what I mean. Evil exploited the people's cowardice and fear. Evil became even bigger than the Black Death itself.

"In 1666 the plague erupted again in Eyam. This time all the wealthy people were gone, safely hidden in their country manors. Only the common folk remained. Predictably, they decided to flee for safety, until the village rector, William Mompesson, spoke up. Knowing that the villagers would spread the disease again, he exhorted them to quarantine themselves in Eyam to save the rest of Derbyshire. A circle was marked out with stones around the town.

172

The Earl of Devonshire agreed to provide most of the necessary food and other goods, which outsiders left nervously on the perimeter every week.

"Figuring that indoor meetings were dangerous, Mompesson moved Sunday worship into a field, where the people could stand some distance from each other. The rector and another minister were the only ones who consistently visited the sick, grieving and dying.

"By the time the plague ran its course, 260 of the 350 villagers had died. One of the last victims was Mompesson's wife. Assuming that he, too, would die, he wrote a farewell letter. It read, in part: 'I thank God, I am content to shake hands with all the world, and I have many comfortable assurances that God will accept me.' He was one of the few to survive."

"Incredible," I said.

"I like him because he had the courage to fight evil," the Sage said. "I can't imagine the agony he felt. People opposed him. Nature turned corrupt. Friends and family died. Cruelty, hatred, fear, superstition and selfishness—it was all there during the Black Death. But here's one man who faced it squarely and refused to be beaten by it."

"It makes me want to be a fighter," I said.

"You'll have plenty of chances," the Sage said. "And it won't be easy."

*   *   *

The What and Where of Evil

No one questions the existence of evil anymore. The evidence is too overwhelming. Even if our personal exposure to it has been limited, a mere glance at the newspaper is enough to show that evil is on a rampage. The Sage mentioned only one of thousands of examples: nature gone crazy; people turned selfish. Evil reigns in the world, consuming our planet.

Still, it is another matter altogether when we discuss its characteristics and origins. What is evil? Where does it come from? How we answer these two questions has serious implications for us. Our answers will determine in a large part how we view discipleship and how we are to address the reality of evil in the world. There is by no means agreement on what the answers are. It appears that there are four alternatives.

First, we can define evil by *categories*. It is a particular movement, organization, nation or person. According to this position, evil is always someone, something or somewhere else; it is never our selves, our causes or our ideas. If anything, we are the very power needed to defeat it.

Such categorical thinking is common. Feminists disparage our sexist society. Conservatives criticize the permissiveness of liberals. Union members complain about the materialism of corporate leaders. Minorities castigate the whites for their tokenism. Whites oppress the blacks, considering them threats or members of an inferior race. Parents question the rebellion of the youth culture. Yet these are not the only evils and not necessarily the worst evils. Thinking so keeps us from seeing how expansive evil is.

We can see the problem. Whomever we condemn does the same thing to us. Whomever we criticize has our ideologies pegged, too. They view us as suspiciously as we view them. Our own categorical thinking about them only reinforces their misapprehensions about us. While capitalists see communists as expansionistic, communists label capitalists as oppressors. Which side we choose to embrace depends as much on indoctrination as it does on careful thinking. Likewise, conservatives view the World Council of Churches warily, saying that it favors Marxist ideology, but liberals often say that fundamentalists are narrow-minded and naive. One is called worldly, the other divisive and self-righteous. Thus evil, always somewhere else, is everywhere and yet nowhere at the same time. Not only is the notion absurd, but it also allows evil to flourish. It keeps us from becoming self-critical, from attacking evil in ourselves first. Thus, while there are evil systems and ideologies, they are not evil in an absolute sense, nor does the evil in them excuse us from seeing and purging the evil in ourselves.

EVIL AND THE PERSONALITY BEHIND IT

Second, evil can also be understood as something exclusively *impersonal*. It is the "system." Social forces, quite beyond our control, are the perpetrators of evil because they create all the oppression in the world. If we could release people from the system's domination, then we could banish evil from the world and live in freedom. Education was once thought to be the great hope of the future because knowledge was considered the sure pathway to liberation. Then it was urban renewal, equal opportunity and social welfare programs. Still later it was modern psychology and the self-help movement. These and other crusades always identify the "system" as the problem. Low self-esteem, laziness, poverty, materialism, crime and oppression would be eliminated if we could figure out how to change the system that causes these things.

Again, there is truth to this. A system can be and often is evil in a way that transcends the evil actions of individuals. The Sage's story about the Black Death points out that evils like prejudice and superstition can create a system that wields power even over individuals, making them do the unthinkable.

But what is the *system*? No one dares to define it concretely. If the system were made up of particular people and specific ideas, then once identified, these evils would become personal and therefore answerable. People would be called to account and have the right to defend themselves. This would lead to discussion, negotiation and accountability. Perhaps we would discover that everyone, including ourselves, must shoulder part of the guilt and take responsibility for the problems of our world.

Blaming a generic "system" is safer because it is conveniently ambiguous. No one is accountable; everyone is the victim. The wealthy and powerful can use the system to excuse their corruption, as many did during the Watergate trials. Leaders of corporations can point to the system to justify their high prices and huge salaries. Politicians can excuse their marginal morality because of the pressure the system puts on them and the compromises inherent in the electoral process. Criminals can blame the system for their chronic deviance.

The problem is that we cannot penetrate and change such an evasive system. It eludes definition and identification. Its impersonal nature lets evil run rampant. And there is nothing we can do about it—unless, of course, we start getting specific and name Judge Walker, Ed Williams, Cousin Mabel, the administration's policy on Latin America or whatever as the source of the problem. But once we identify particular people and ideas, *we* too may be called into question. Who wants that?

Third, we can view evil through the philosophy of *moral relativism.* This can arise either from skepticism—which denies the existence of absolutes, making morality arbitrary—or from monism—which sees good and evil as false distinctions that must be transcended—or from some forms of dualism—which view good and evil as equal competitors with history telling the story of their inconclusive war. So whether it is because we cannot identify right or wrong, or because right and wrong do not actually exist, or because it doesn't matter which we choose, the outcome is the same: morality becomes relative.

We can observe the malaise of relativity in modern society. We have lost our capacity to resist evil because we do not know what it is anymore. One person's evil is often another person's good, and vice versa. Who therefore will decide what is right and wrong? A Gandhi? A Lincoln? Jesus Christ? Probably not. If relativism is in fact an accurate view of reality, Stalin and Mao are the men to follow. Might makes right. The moral climate of the world will be determined on the battlefield, not in the courtroom, university or church. Relativists cannot sidestep the problem of the lack of an absolute good in their system.

Finally, evil can be defined in *personal* terms. It is not an "it" at all; it is personal. This is the biblical and logical answer. Seeing the nature of evil any other way is illogical, impractical and dangerous. Either people accuse everyone else of promulgating evil and excuse themselves, thereby setting its boundaries everywhere and yet nowhere; or an ambigious, ubiquitous system constitutes evil, and no one can penetrate it; or good and evil are equals in conflict, and the outcome of their battle is uncertain and morally relative. In any case, evil itself is never unmasked and expunged. It is free to continue its domination.

Christianity teaches that *personality* is at the center of the universe. A transcendent, personal God reigns, and he has created personality as the highest manifestation of his own being. Personal consciousness, volition, communicativeness and creativity are the supreme realities of life as God created it. Both goodness and evil follow this pattern of personality. As goodness is willed by people who trust in God, so evil is willed by those who defy him. In their pride they attempt to usurp his throne and pervert his creation. Evil's source is in the person. Jesus said, "For from within, out of the heart of man, come evil thoughts, fornication, theft, murder, adultery, coveting, wickedness, deceit, licentiousness, envy, slander, pride, foolishness. All these evil things come from within, and they defile a man" (Mk 7:21-23). Thus evil is personal, not merely systemic; it is somewhere in particular, not just everywhere. It is powerful and insidious, but it is not absolute. God still rules; good will triumph; evil will be banished forever from the world.

The Bible also teaches that because of man's choice to pursue evil over good, evil has become rooted in the world itself. While we are still responsible, there is a sense in which evil is greater than mere human expression can account for. The whole world has turned corrupt. Ideologies, structures, causes and nations can manifest great evil. Manmade structures, however good they were in their inception, can become tools of evil and slaves of the demonic. Hitler's Germany and Stalin's Russia are examples of such evil. Paul calls these institutions and ideas the "principalities and powers." They are demonically controlled social structures, created by man, yet ruling over man at the same time.

But the Bible says more. It says that the conflict between good and evil is not only and primarily human and structural, but it is also, and more fundamentally, spiritual. On the fringes of the spiritual universe is a being, also created by God, who once maneuvered to dethrone God; he failed in his attempt and fled for safety from God's presence. He is now hell-bent on disrupting God's scheme for life by deceiving, tempting, accusing and holding in bondage men and women. He wants to lure the crown of creation away from God. He purposes to oppose God's plan to create new persons, a new community and a new world. He aims to deprive us of grace and quench the Spirit's work within us. He wants to exploit our pride and drive us not only away from God but also into some terrible bondage. Thus, although evil's influence finds hospitality in the human heart and ready access into groups and systems, its ultimate origin is a rebellious and ruthless being, Satan, who is the personality behind all evil.

The Deceiver

Satan is a deceiver. He calls into question the goodness, sovereignty and wisdom of God. He wants us to doubt God's goodness, that he will not do what is best for us; or God's sovereignty, that he is not able to do what is best for us; or God's wisdom, that he does not know what is best for us. That is indeed Satan's fundamental strategy. After Eve had told the serpent about the only prohibition of the garden and the consequences of violating it, he said to her: "You will not die. For God knows that when you eat of it your eyes will be opened, and you will be like God, knowing good and evil" (Gen 3:4-5). God, he implied, was threatened by Adam and Eve. He was afraid of competitors and unwilling to give them the best. He was therefore unworthy of their trust and obedience. If they wanted real life, they would have to abandon him and find it for themselves.

Deception has an appealing logic to it. If indeed God is *not* good, sovereign and wise, then we simply *must* take matters into our own hands and strive to squeeze a little bit of happiness out of life. Once we begin wondering about God's desire to make us fruitful, for example, we will eventually fall prey to ambition. Once we suspect God's plan to give us true pleasure, we will slide into lust. Once we question God's ability to make us content, we will grow envious and greedy. If we doubt God's goodness, sovereignty and wisdom,

Satan will find an empty corner in our hearts and spin an insidious and suffocating web of delusion and rebellion. We will strive for independence from God, something we were never meant to have.

Satan deceives us, however, not only by perverting our view of God, but also by distorting our view of creation. By challenging God's lordship over the world and the rules God has established for its proper governance (see chapter eighteen), Satan deprives creation of its ultimate reference point. Thus creation becomes an idol to worship or a thing to exploit. It is exalted or debased, but never respected as a trust given by a good Creator to his stewards.

Consider the outcome. Once Satan causes us to doubt God, he can turn our hearts to the world, where we must find happiness apart from God. But since our appetite for happiness is insatiable, we ravage the created order just trying to satisfy our hunger (the Bible calls it "idolatry"). Marriage, careers, wealth, nature, sex are misused and then abused in a vain effort to find life. But how quickly our craving returns. Enough never ends up being enough. Satan is always baiting us to take one more step. "Next time you'll be satisfied," he promises. But notice: it is never now, it is always "next time." Thus lust leads to perversion, the hunger for security to crass materialism, desires for modest success to ambition and greed. The good world is forced to deliver more than it is able, and so its goodness is corrupted.

Evil is dealt with most effectively, then, by discerning how true goodness has been perverted. Jealousy is love ruined by possessiveness. Envy is an exaggerated appreciation for another's talents and disparagement of one's own. Promiscuity is sexual privilege without personal responsibility. Violence is anger expressed inappropriately or justice pursued apart from the state's authority. Ambition is desire for success without the discipline of servanthood. These are good things gone bad. The world, created to teem with beauty and excellence, has been twisted but not beyond repair. It can still be enjoyed for what it was meant to be.

Once we acknowledge that God is God, we are free to explore the world and enjoy its goodness. Thomas Merton writes:

A saint is capable of loving created things and enjoying the use of them and dealing with them in a perfectly simple, natural manner, making no formal references to God, drawing no attention to his own piety, and acting without an artificial rigidity at all. His gentleness and his sweetness are not pressed through his pores by the crushing restraint of a spiritual strait-jacket. They come from his direct docility to the light of truth and to the will of God.

When we are one with God's love, we own all things in Him. They are ours to offer Him in Christ His Son, for all things belong to the sons of God and we are Christ's and Christ is God's. Resting in His glory above all pleasure and pain, joy or sorrow, and every other good or evil, we love in all things His will rather than the things themselves, and that is the way we make creation a sacrifice in praise of God.[25]

In combating evil, therefore, we should reject very few things categorically. Religious systems tend to create prohibitions. They tell us *what not to do* but not *what to do* to reclaim what Satan has encroached upon. Negative religion gives Satan an authority that he does not deserve. It hands part of the world to him as if he had some kind of inherent right to its domination and ownership.

The consequences of such legalism are disastrous. We live in a good world; and we were created with the capacities to enjoy it. Yet many forms of the Christian religion have no positive worldliness in them. They undermine the truth that we were made to live in the world, thus leaving people to face a world their religion has abandoned. Many people have been told that participation in and enjoyment of the world are under Satan's domain. In their minds worldly pleasure and evil are the same, however sharply that departs from true Christianity. Since they have never been taught the ability to morally discriminate, an ability that true Christianity cultivates, many explore all worldly mediums—film, theater, dance, business, sports, entertainment—uncritically and unabashedly, especially if they are reacting against an oppressive religious past. Others, and there are few who can endure it for long, retreat from the world altogether. Both outcomes are tragic.

Jesus was called a glutton and a drunkard, a friend of the wanton and wasted. He loved life, and he associated with the people who, however worldly, knew how to embrace life wholeheartedly. Jesus had joy, even to the bitter end. His living established a new spirit in religion. He did not reject and prohibit; he affirmed and embraced. Jesus was known not by what he did not do but by what he did, by his good deeds (Mk 3:1-6). The world, he said, was a good place. Corruption came not from the world itself but from the hearts of men and women (Mk 7:18-23).

Even Paul, that most severe and zealous of disciples, argued that creation was good. He disagreed with both the libertine and the religious fanatic. He struck a middle course: the world was made for man; it was to be enjoyed and cared for, not idolized or rejected.

Now the Spirit expressly says that in later times some will depart from the faith by giving heed to deceitful spirits and doctrines of demons, through the pretensions of liars whose consciences are seared, who forbid marriage and enjoy abstinence from foods which God created to be received with thanksgiving by those who believe and know the truth. For everything created by God is good, and nothing is to be rejected if it is received with thanksgiving; for then it is consecrated by the word of God and prayer. (1 Tim 4:1-5)

Satan is called the deceiver in the Scriptures, the father of lies (Jn 8:44). We can counter his influence, then, by affirming the truth about God—that he is good, sovereign and wise—and by taking pleasure in and responsibility for his creation. We can combat deception only by overcoming doubt and rejecting idolatry.

The Tempter

Once deceived, we are vulnerable to temptation. It plagues us when we yearn for something we do not have but see the possibility of getting. Temptation does not affect the satiated. It can only enter a vacuum, when we feel a chasm between desire and fulfillment, emptiness and satisfaction. Only a hungry man is tempted by food; only a lusting person by sex; only a lonely person by false friendship. Thus desire joins doubt, and the two become the companions of temptation. Doubt turns us away from God; desire makes us the slave of our appetites; and temptation provides the possibility of fulfillment *now*.

Desires in themselves are not evil. We shall never overcome temptation by suppressing our desires or by pretending they do not exist. They become evil only when we satisfy them unrighteously or when we refuse to wait for God himself to fulfill them. God rarely says no in absolute terms. He is more likely to say, "No, not now, but later," or "Not in this way, but that way." Temptation therefore plays upon reasonable desire. That makes it easy to yield to. It feels natural and right, and it is easily justified. "Doesn't God want me to have this or do that? Of course he does. He wants the best for me."

But what Satan offers is merely disguised as the best. Only God can give what is truly the best. Waiting, and thus postponing the satisfaction of immediate desires, prepares us to receive God's best, which is not only worldly pleasure but also intimacy with him.

Consider Jesus' temptation (Lk 4). Satan tempted him first by appealing to his physical needs and desires (the "lust of the flesh"— 1 Jn 2:16). This temptation appealed to a reasonable desire, but Jesus refused to yield because he believed that there were matters more important than his immediate needs. "Man shall not live by bread alone." We must never let Satan reduce us to being a mere collage of lusts and appetites.

Satan also tempted Jesus with earthly powers (the "lust of the eyes"). This is the temptation of justifying questionable means to achieve godly ends, of usurping powers for the self with the justification that we are doing it for others or even for God. It is the temptation of striving for self-advancement, not servanthood; superiority, not submission. Satan wants us to bow to his methods. We think that once we have gained power his way, we can use it God's way. It is the temptation of compromise. So Jesus shunned Satan, "You shall worship the Lord, and him only shall you serve."

Finally, Satan tempted Jesus with self-serving religion (the "pride of life"). This is the ultimate temptation, for God himself is made a servant to our desires. Satan wanted Jesus to force God to do a miracle. He tempted Jesus to put God under his control in order to prove that God is really God. Jesus responded, "You shall never tempt God." Let God, in other words, define who he is, determine what he must do and decide when he must do it.

Jesus resisted, Satan fled, and eventually something remarkable happened. Satan tempted Jesus to turn stone into bread; later, Jesus fed 5,000 with a few loaves and fishes. Satan tempted Jesus with power; Jesus was later exalted to the right hand of God, far above all powers. Satan tempted Jesus with self-serving religion; later, Jesus raised a man from the dead. Satan fans immediate desires; God asks us to wait for his best. He is the master of timing, the Giver of every perfect gift. He wills to make us Christlike, and he gives us the grace and the Spirit to accomplish that.

The Accuser

Before falling to temptation, we are enticed by a devil wearing a gossamer gown, speaking in a sensual voice and smelling like a rose in bloom. But after we yield to temptation, Satan reappears as a heartless lawyer seeking to strap us into the electric chair. As the tempter, he wants us to presume upon God's mercy and disregard his justice. As the accuser, he seeks to deprive us of mercy and drive us to judgment.

In the courtroom Satan thunders, "How *dare* you ask for mercy, you who are so double-minded and weak. Consider how many times you have sinned! Will you presume upon God now by asking for his forgiveness again for a sin you have committed a hundred times before? No mercy for you, sinner. You deserve only judgment."

There is no law in Satan's world when he tempts us and no grace when he accuses us. During the time of temptation Satan has us believe in a weak God, one who is too naive and stupid to understand that we could do anything wrong. After we yield to temptation, the accuser sends us to a ruthless judge who takes the law and beats us with it. Satan allows only two responses; despair or high-minded resolutions. In the former case he tries to persuade us that giving up on ourselves is the same thing as giving up on God. He wants us to confuse our despair with God's judgment, our guilt with God's rejection. In the latter case Satan is pleased when we concentrate so much on our efforts that we cannot see the bounty of God's grace extended to us. He wants us to confuse our sincerity and hard work with God's forgiveness. Surprisingly, Satan even applauds our resolutions, because promises, made to God when we feel guilty, never provide enough motivation to make us obedient to God when the guilt dissipates. Satan wants us to think that we can earn God's forgiveness by pledging that we will "never do it again," for he knows that, relying on our own will, we will do it again. And again. And again.

Bondage and Freedom
Satan's ultimate goal is to put us into bondage to anything but God. He wants to make us slaves to sin, which will make us his slaves as well. As the deceiver he wants us to think that we can live independently from God, even flirt with sin and still maintain some control over our lives. He does not want us to know that the one choice we have in life is who will be our master (Rom 6:13-18).

Bondage to sin has three dimensions. The first is *choice*. We choose to be bound to bitterness, appetites, the opinions of people, the immediate, ambition and even darkness. This is the most observable dimension of the three, since it manifests itself behaviorally in rebellion, addiction, vanity, moral compromise, fanaticism, selfishness and the like. Such choices are made out of pride.

Second is the dimension of *propensity*. Our pasts—family influences, painful experiences, heredity, peer pressure—determine to a great degree the path down which our sinful choices will take us. Modern psychology can help us here, not in explaining away sinful behavior but in explaining why our sin manifests itself as it does— for example, why one person is rebellious and another lazy.

There is, finally, the dimension of *demonic influence.* Satan exploits our pride and makes us a prisoner to it. He takes away our freedom. He pins us down and locks us in chains so that we cannot escape. He looks for vulnerabilities in our defense. He turns sinful choices into habits.

The Sage told the story about William Mompesson, one of the few in plague-ridden England who had the courage to fight evil. He not only fought the evil of the Black Death but also of people's selfish responses. He is a good example for us because he did not use evil circumstances to excuse evil behavior. Mompesson took personal responsibility. He dared to stand above.

We, too, are responsible to resist evil. While it is more powerful than we are, God is more powerful than it is. If we repent of our will for evil (our pride) and turn to God for protection and power, then the evil in ourselves, in the world and in the Evil One himself will be defeated. It will take time, of course. The war will not be won until Christ returns, when he will put all of God's enemies under his feet. But victory is assured even now. This we must believe and so choose to submit to the Master who stands as Lord of all. Then, with Mompesson, we will be content to shake hands with the world, and we will have many comfortable assurances that God will welcome us into his kingdom.

Study Questions
1. Take a few minutes and think about the evils in the world today. We live in the most advanced of cultures, and yet there is so much evil. How can you explain this?
2. The chapter contained four alternative ways of defining evil: categorical, impersonal, relativistic and personal. Can you think of some concrete examples that show how the first three explanations are used today and why they are inadequate alternatives?
3. According to Genesis 3:1-7 and Luke 4:1-13 how does Satan tempt us?
4. Satan perverts the good. Think about some examples of evil as a perversion of the good. How can you overcome evil in your life by affirming and doing what is good?

VI
SAINT-MAKING

This section is the most practical. It explains in concrete terms how we can live as disciples. It is also the last section, and well it should be. By now it should be obvious that God is at the heart of discipleship. God must be the source; he must provide the direction; he must give us power.

Still, there are human dimensions. Responsiveness implies cooperation. God calls us, for example, to discern and do his will, not only in the future but also in the present (chapter sixteen). Further, he summons us to become spiritually disciplined by assuming postures to receive what God offers (chapter seventeen). He also commands us to obey him by learning to live with the logical implications of his goodness, sovereignty and wisdom (chapter eighteen). Finally, God calls us to discern how the life of discipleship naturally expands, affecting all areas of life and reclaiming the world for the kingdom (chapter nineteen). These are human dimensions because they require human volition. But they follow from the divine dimensions of discipleship we explored in the previous sections.

Chapter 16

GUIDANCE
AND
FREEDOM

IN THE BEGINNING OF AUGUST the Sage and I drove about forty
miles north to a secluded forest where we planned to hike for a day.
We wanted to escape the encroaching civilization, and we didn't care
to meet a dozen or so people or cross any more asphalt roads. We
wanted to know that there were still places that were untainted by
human presence. Of course the forest we were visiting had seen
humans before—thousands, I'm sure. But it had that primitive and
secluded air about it.

We drove to the edge of it, found a marked path and plunged into
a stand of oak, birch, maple and a few clumps of lovely pines. The
forest floor was covered with ferns. The day was warm and sunny,

but the canopy of trees shaded the path and made our hike crisp and refreshing.

We had planned to walk about five miles to a small waterfall, where we would rest, swim and eat lunch. After a half-hour, however, we came to a triple fork in the path with no sign in sight to indicate which of the three would lead us to the waterfall. I figured that the Sage knew, and so I asked him.

"Well, which one do we take?"

"I don't know," he said. "I thought you knew where we were going."

So there we stood, staring at the three paths, wondering which one to choose. We were quiet for a few minutes. I finally decided to search for a marker that might be hidden or fallen, but I found nothing.

"What do we do now?" I asked.

"Suppose," said the Sage, "that only one of these three paths leads to the waterfall. What would you do?"

"I'm not sure," I said. "I'd probably guess as best as I could and then start walking again."

"Do you think you'd enjoy the hike?" he asked.

I thought about his question for a moment. "No," I said. "I'd be thinking all the time about whether or not it was the right one."

"Exactly," he said. "You'd never know until you spotted the waterfall or walked another four or five miles in vain and ended up somewhere else. Now let's say that every one of these paths leads to the place we want to go. Which would you take then?"

"It wouldn't make any difference," I said. "I guess I'd take the one that appealed to me the most—that one," and I pointed to the one that ascended a hill covered with pine trees. "The view would be excellent. And I like pine trees."

"Let's go then," he said. "You blaze the trail."

"But is it the right path?" I asked.

"Yes, I think so. In fact, I'm sure of it. If only one of the paths went to the waterfall, there'd be a sign to tell us so. Forest rangers always make it clear when they need to. As it is, there's no sign.

So I'm sure all of them end up at the same place. You lead the way."

*   *   *

Freedom with Guarantees

There is freedom in discipleship. Once we decide to pursue the goal of discipleship, it is impossible to choose pathways that will guide us to fruitless and false destinations. In the long run we simply cannot fail. Discipleship gives us the freedom to be confident, for we know that our future is securely in God's hands. It also liberates us to make bold decisions, for we know that our present options, however many there are, will all lead to fruitfulness. Discipleship, in other words, gives us the freedom to do the will of God—*now*. To understand such freedom, we must first explore what we mean by the will of God.

God's will for our lives logically follows God's drama for history. The one sets the context for the other. History shows us the broad outlines of what God has done and will do in the world. God's will for our lives represents the fine wording of how we must respond in the present. The drama is spectacular, the will is specific; the drama is powerful, the will is practical. Thus the two are inextricably bound up together. The drama shows us where we are going, but God must first tell us how to get there.

I have always had problems figuring out God's will. I suspect that you have, too. Life sometimes feels like a huge maze that has so many options leading to dead ends that we despair of ever finding a way out. Decisions concerning education, careers, marriage, children, involvements and responsibilities loom over us. Choosing between equally attractive options for, let's say, a job change is bad enough. Determining which is God's will is worse.

I hate to make decisions. I make them very slowly, and I often doubt the wisdom of my decisions even after I make them. Before I moved to my present job, I had three opportunities from which to choose. By the time I decided to move to where I am now, my wife and friends were ready to send me anywhere, as long as it was away from them!

It bothered me that finding God's will caused such anxiety. That did not feel right to me theologically. I wondered why he would make it so perplexing. I believed that God had enough problems persuading us to *do* his will. Why would he create still another by making it hard to find?

I also noticed that whenever I wanted to discover God's will, I usually neglected to obey the general commandments I already knew. The obsession to find God's will on one matter made me neglect the others. My preoccupation made me a poor husband, minister and friend.

Missing the Bull's Eye

So I began to review what I considered to be the traditional model of understanding God's will. I realized that in most Christian communities we are taught to ask the question, How can I discern God's will? That very question sends us on a journey. We are supposed to search for God's will, which is presumably "out there" someplace. Life is made adventurous and risky, not by doing God's will but by finding it.

According to the traditional model, God's will is always some future option numbered among several. It is the one career we must choose from the many that interest us; it is the marriage partner we must find among all the members of the opposite sex we know; it is the one activity we must schedule on some Friday night, though there are many we *could* schedule. Since we can choose only one of them, we must figure out how to eliminate all but the right one. So we pray; we seek advice from friends; we weigh the options carefully; we read books; we fast; we look for signs. We do anything that will aid us in our deliberations.

Of course we must eventually make a decision. But what if we choose the wrong one? Will we ever be able to get back on track, or will we be outside of God's will forever? These are not academic questions. Many Christians believe they will miss the will of God if they choose a wrong option, even though they have no reliable way of knowing which is the right one.

This popular model causes some problems. For one, it makes us ask the wrong question, How can I find God's will? Did God hide it somewhere? Is he withholding it to confuse us? Does he want to be evasive and unclear? Hardly! God's will is not a treasure buried in the future, found only if we dig for it in the right place (God only knows where). Of all matters about which God wants to be clear, his will is certainly one of them. God has enough difficulty inspiring us to do his will; he is not so foolish to make his will hard to find.

God's will is not to be sought; it is to be obeyed (Eph 4; Col 3). If finding God's will were a crucial issue, Scripture would speak to it. Yet the Bible is silent on the matter. It speaks not about finding God's will but about doing his will. We busy ourselves so often with matters concerning career, marriage, education and other future plans that we disregard the simple will of God which is known to us through the Bible and which requires us to obey him now. It is misleading, then, to ask, How can I find the will of God? It is better to ask, Am I doing the will of God I already know? God's will is clear where it needs to be.

Another problem with the popular model is that it teaches us a false view of God. If God is our Father, how can we make him the author of a will we may never know? Is it really possible to miss God's will after we consider who God is? Yes, if we are indifferent or disobedient but not if we desire to please him. God is not aloof from the affairs of daily life. He is not like the capricious gods of Olympus whose desires were clear one moment and confusing the next. "Seek first his kingdom and his righteousness, and all these things shall be yours as well. Therefore do not be anxious about tomorrow, for tomorrow will be anxious for itself. Let the day's own trouble be sufficient for the day" (Mt 6:33-34). God's will is a reflection of God himself. Both are accessible to us.

Finally, the popular model betrays our American obsession with having to figure everything out. Real life for many of us is an untainted past and an organized future, both encompassing a present which is sterile and stagnant because it is too safe. We want to know too much, to the point where security replaces adventure.

The Bible, however, invites us to embark on a journey whose final destination is made certain only by the One who leads us. Sadly, we refuse to join the host of pilgrims unless we have a detailed map in hand. We betray our lack of confidence in God by following the shortest and easiest route between the beginning and end of the journey. We rarely consider that the surest route is not necessarily the shortest and straightest. It is often circuitous, more like a drive in the Rockies than like one in Nebraska. Maps are not nearly as reliable as a good Guide.

The Way of Wisdom and Love

The great commandments sum up God's will: love God with heart, soul, mind and strength, and love your neighbor as yourself. It is as simple as that. We are to pursue the life of discipleship, as Jesus interpreted it in the Sermon on the Mount. Reduced to its most basic form, it is love (Rom 13:8-10; 1 Cor 13).

But what about the future? God commands us to obey him in what we already know, however sharp or blurry the future is to us. The present, in other words, matters more than the future. Yet, if we live obediently, we gain the liberty to make bold decisions concerning the future without wondering whether or not they are in God's will. They will be, every time. If we choose to pursue discipleship, it is impossible to miss the will of God.

In the traditional model there may be two equally good options. We must therefore decide which one is God's will. Since we have no sure way of knowing, uncertainty hangs over us, even after we make our decisions. In the new model, however, the choice is not between the two options. The real choice is between obedience and disobedience. If we choose the pathway of discipleship, the narrow and hard path Jesus followed, then we are free to choose whatever is consistent with that pathway. We may have four equally good options, and we are free to choose any of them. We have the *liberty* of choosing and the *security* of knowing we will never miss the will of God. By pursuing discipleship, we cannot lose.

The will of God, then, should not be limited to a few specific concerns, as most of our decisions are. It is comprehensive. Discipleship envelops all of life. Once we are within its orbit, our present and future are settled. "If God is for us, who can be against us? . . . Nothing can separate us from the love of God." Furthermore, God's will should not be reduced to a decision over many options. Rather, it requires a decision over direction. *The* question in life is not, Should I take a job in Chicago or one in Los Angeles? It is, Will I set my heart toward kingdom living, regardless of where I live and what I do? (Eph 5:15-17).

By now a question looms in our minds. Does God have a specific will for our futures? Can we be sure that he has *one* person for us to marry, *one* job for us to do, *one* college for us to attend or *one* responsibility for us to fulfill? And if he does, then how can we find out what it is?

God has one will for us, but in two very different ways. On the one hand, God's will is *predetermined.* God dwells in eternity. Every moment of time is the present to him. He is just as aware of the future ten years from now as he is of today. He created and controls time. He not only knows what we and everybody else will be doing five and fifteen and a hundred years from now, but he has also willed it to be so, all of it. The world's destiny has been designed by God. He determines the course of history.

But we do not dwell in eternity; we live in time and space. We cannot see as God sees. He knows that even better than we do. He does not expect us to understand the future from eternity's perspective—not completely anyway. Thus, he has also revealed his will to us as an *ideal,* a portrait of what we can become. It is a wonderful, albeit exacting, pathway down which we can march. It is something we can and must choose.

Suppose that you have observed a novelist for over a year while she was writing a novel whose story spans several decades. She molds the plot; she creates the characters. Finally she puts it all down on paper. When you read the novel, however, you sense that it has a life of its own. Though the plot takes sudden and unexpected turns, it seems to make logical sense, as if it had to have happened that way. The characters seem to be real. They make good and bad decisions; they are both victims of fate and shapers of their futures. You know, of course, that the author wrote the novel. It is the product of her mind, entirely. Yet the novel, within itself, seems to have its own kind of integrity and inevitability. It is very much alive.

That is the paradox of eternity and history. God dwells in eternity, controls time and directs history. He has written the novel of history, every word of it. But he wrote the novel in such a way that, although he is the author and we are only the characters, it allows us to shape our own futures. We have freedom. We can, if we wish, embrace the ideal life available to us in him, or we can carve out some meager life for ourselves, in defiance of God, even though we are bound to fail if we do. In one sense, then, God shapes every movement and turn in human history; his will is predetermined. Yet in another sense we make very real choices. His will is also an ideal we can choose to follow or reject. Both are true.

Still, we are avoiding the inevitable question. Does God have one pathway in mind for us to follow? Yes, he does. Can we discover it? Yes, we can: first, by pursuing discipleship, because that is the ideal taught clearly in Scripture; second, by believing boldly that eternity has entered into history in Jesus Christ, and not only into history but also into us who know him. His life has been taken up into ours and ours into his and both into God's. Hence, as long as we strive to be disciples, we will always choose the pathway that pleases God. That is the freedom of having eternity's Son living in our hearts.

Pursuing discipleship as our primary goal, and as God's primary will, directs our efforts toward those ends most valuable to God. That is why the Bible draws our attention to the general characteristics of discipleship. Character and convictions, hospitality and diligence should take precedence over such matters as occupation and marriage. Our occupations, however diverse, require true character if we want to succeed in them. Marriage needs love for its growth and stability. God wants to harness our energies so that, whatever our interests and occupations, we will do them well and honor him.

This new model, furthermore, highlights what in Scripture is the most important moment for our lives—the present (2 Cor 6:1-2). God has redeemed our past. He promises to smile on our future. He waits for us to seek him in the present. Thomas Kelly calls it the "Holy Now."

Instead of anxiety about our pasts, our past defects, our long-standing deficiencies blight our well-intentioned future efforts, all our past sense of weakness falls away and we stand erect, in this Holy Now, joyous, serene, assured, unafraid. Between the relinquished past and the untrodden future stands this Holy Now, whose bulk has swelled to cosmic size, for within the Now is the dwelling place of God himself. In the Now we are at home at last. The fretful winds of time are stilled, the nostalgic longings of this heaven-born earth-traveler come to rest.[26]

This eternal moment draws into itself our past and future, all of time, in order to show us that it is only in this very moment that we can meet the living God and do his will.

We also benefit by discovering the simplicity of life. By concentrating on discipleship, our minds become uncluttered, our hearts untangled, our wills disengaged from too many demands. Simplicity of life, having very few but all-important concerns, releases us from having to arrange our lives like many people organize a wedding, every detail ponderously and systematically laid out. We can give ourselves to the few essentials that make life wonderful.

'Tis a gift to be simple,
'Tis a gift to be free,
'Tis a gift to come down where you ought to be.
And when you find yourself in the place just right,
'Twill be in the valley of love and delight.

When true simplicity is gained,
To bow and to bend we shan't be ashamed.

To turn, turn will be our delight
Till by turning, turning we come round right.

By pursuing the kingdom, we also discover the true freedom of the
Christian faith. We have no doubt heard it said many times, "I
married unwisely and missed God's will for my life"; or, "I chose the
wrong career and am therefore out of God's will." This perspective
betrays a dangerously narrow view of God. There are consequences
to bad decisions, of course, and God disciplines us for the bad choices
we make. But once we return to him, we are immediately thrust
into the center of his will. Thus a Christian woman who married
an unbelieving husband disobeyed God; but if she repents, she
moves once more into the current of God's will. God will build
strength into the marriage she entered unwisely. A man who chose
a career for the sake of money violated God's will; but if he returns
to God, he also returns to God's will. God will use the career he
pursued so greedily for some good purpose. We can never ultimately miss the will of God. God's grace is just too great.

Finally, this new model pushes us toward another kind of freedom, the freedom of living boldly. Discipleship allows us to take
risks, to live adventurously, to explore the drama of being a Christian in the world. We have no need for horoscopes, hot-water
bottles, parachutes, pills, a Farmer's Almanac or a twenty-four-
hour deodorant on the journey God wants us to take. We have no
need to be safe because we know we cannot lose. We can choose
life, recklessly (and wisely) welcoming the many options we have
to serve God. Jesus called it the abundant life. It is the freedom
of discipleship.

I want to do things to be doing them. . . .
I don't want to do nice things for people so that I will be "nice."
I don't want to work to make money,
I want to work to work.
Today I don't want to live for,
I want to live.[27]

Study Questions

1. Have you ever had to make a difficult decision that utterly mystified you? How did you respond? How did you go about figuring out God's will?

2. What are some of the popular ways of discovering God's will? What is helpful in these? What potential problems do they have?

3. What do you learn about God's will from Ephesians 5:15-17, Matthew 6:25-34 and Romans 12:2?

4. What are some of the benefits of *assuming* we will be in God's will if we simply set our hearts to obey him?

5. Do you need to make any big decisions right now? What guidelines should you use? Do you dare to believe that you can't miss God's will?

Chapter 17

SPIRITUAL
DISCIPLINES

IN AUGUST MY PARENTS, the Sage and I drove to the Grand Traverse Bay to view the yachts in the marina and to watch the regatta. It was an annual event for us and one that always fascinated me. Sailing requires a great deal of skill and grace. It matches two forces—wind and wits—that work with each other one moment and against each other the next. The outcome is always unpredictable.

The weather disappointed us. Never had we seen such a hot, humid day. Worse yet, there was no wind. The boats inched their way through the races. On one occasion a comical crew took a fan on board, hooked it up to batteries and pointed it toward the sail. They drew the applause and laughter of everyone on shore. Later, another crew took down the jib and, in its place, hoisted a sign that read, "Cabin Cruisers have more fun."

Eventually I tired of watching, and so I left my parents and strolled with the Sage through the marina. Hundreds of boats, many of extraordinary size and design, lined the docks. We were in the center of Michigan's opulence. I was overwhelmed and intrigued by what I saw. I began to wonder what it would be like to travel the high seas and visit famous ports.

"If there's one place you could visit by boat," I asked the Sage, just as we had stopped to admire The Queen Bee, a forty-foot sailboat, "where would it be?"

"New Zealand," he said. "I've always wanted to visit that island. How about you?"

"Someplace exotic, like a port on the island of Madagascar," I said.

"What kind of boat would you choose?"

"A sailboat, of course," I said.

"Why?"

"Who would want to gas up all the time? Besides, there's something exciting about being out there on the high seas with nothing but the wind and water. I like the effortlessness of it. Motors take the adventure out of it."

"Suppose you were sitting in the middle of the Indian Ocean and had no wind for days. What would you do?" he asked.

"I'd keep the sails hoisted and wait."

"Nothing else?"

"I don't think so," I said. "It's the wind or nothing. Sailors must be patient. But when the wind blows, how wonderful to race along under its power."

*　　　　　*　　　　　*

The Problem with Discipline
"*Train* yourself in godliness," Paul wrote to Timothy. "For while bodily training is of some value, godliness is of value in every way, as it holds promise for the present life and also for the life to come. The saying is sure and worthy of full acceptance. For to this end we *toil* and *strive*, because we have our hope set on the living God"

(1 Tim 4:7-10). Paul practiced spiritual discipline, and he expected others to do the same. He often employed the terminology of athletics (1 Cor 9:24-27; 2 Tim 4:7) to teach that the Christian faith requires effort and practice. It is necessary to be disciplined if we want to progress in discipleship.

But to many of us discipline is a nuisance and sometimes a curse. It burdens us as often as it helps us. Guilt, not growth, and legalism, not liberty, result from our attempts to be disciplined. Mention the word and more often than not you will observe one of two reactions: depression from those who have tried and failed or self-righteousness from those who have tried and succeeded. Worship, Bible study, prayer—these exercises make us either flagellate or congratulate ourselves, but rarely do they help us forget about ourselves as we sail under the wind of God's grace.

What has gone wrong? If spiritual discipline is defined as little more than ordinary discipline, only with different exercises and goals, then it will hinder us. Not that ordinary discipline is bad. Often it is very helpful. Spiritual discipline, however, is different.

Ordinary discipline is what we practice to achieve some earthly goal—a means to a particular end: victory in competition, increased sales, being more efficient or whatever. For this kind of discipline the resources and motivation must come from within ourselves (ability, desire and effort) and from our circumstances (luck, timing, a hospitable audience, favorable judges). Thus if a tennis player wants to reach the finals of the Wimbledon tennis tournament, he must work very hard, possess outstanding talent and pay a lot of money to hire a good coach; he must also hope for a propitious draw so that he plays the weaker players first. Likewise, a musician who wants acclaim must practice long hours and take lessons from a master. If she has sufficient talent and drive, and if she is in the right place at the right time, then maybe she will be able to break into the elite group of musicians who concertize as a career.

That is the problem with ordinary discipline. It is risky. Many of us never develop discipline because we are afraid of disappointment and failure. If we try as hard as we can, push ourselves as far as we can and practice as long as we can, then we must be willing to accept our limitations as well as enjoy our triumphs. We might *not* break the world record. We might *not* earn first chair. We might *not* look thin although we have lost as much weight as we can. We might *not* earn an A. We will have to say to ourselves, "This is the best I can do, and it doesn't seem very good." Who wants to make such an admission? It is safer to be lazy or fail at a task or only imagine what we could achieve if we were lucky, than to be disciplined, succeed only modestly and thus have to acknowledge that we are no better than average. Sometimes lack of discipline protects us from facing our limitations.

Even if we do succeed, we rarely stay content for long. When ascending a ladder it is natural to look up, not down—to see how much higher we could go, not how high we have already climbed. When we reach one goal, we usually set another. Discipline, then, rarely satisfies our hunger for achievement. If anything, it only increases the appetite.

Ordinary discipline also creates another serious problem: imbalance. If by chance we do discover something we are good at, we tend to exploit that strength, push ourselves to the limit and disregard other parts of our humanity also needing attention. If there is a little piece of the world we can claim all to ourselves, why not do it? It is satisfying to our egos to be big fish in little ponds, big kings in little kingdoms. Some athletes, for example, refine their physical prowess but slight their minds; some musicians master an instrument but neglect their bodies; some businessmen make millions but lack charity. Too often discipline undermines the wholeness of our humanity.

Spiritual discipline can do that, too. If treated as an end in itself—for instance, as the primary characteristic of being Christian—then it will make us as one-dimensional as ordinary discipline tends to. Christianity will become all effort and no grace. Our discipline will end up shutting God out by replacing him with legalism, which causes either guilt or self-righteousness. Our discipline will become a curse to us.

Opening the Sails

Spiritual discipline also has a goal, but it is attainable only by God's grace. Spiritual discipline is not like ordinary discipline. Although it still takes hard work, it does not function as the primary means of reaching the goal. This is because when we use spiritual discipline, we first acknowledge the existence of the God who rules the universe, who has revealed himself in Jesus Christ and who purposes to make us like himself. If God is God, if he is truly good, then *our* reaching up to him is not nearly as important as *his* reaching down to us. The movement is always in our direction. That completely alters the nature of spiritual discipline.

The goal of such discipline is not to *earn* anything, but to *receive* what God offers. Our efforts, however necessary they are, do not matter as much as his. He is committed to us and wants to give us life. Spiritual discipline puts us in a posture to receive what he freely offers. Practicing spiritual discipline is like cupping our hands to drink from a cold mountain stream. The posture is important, but the refreshment comes from the water, not from the hands themselves. Cupped hands and an open mouth are channels to get the water from the stream into the mouth. That is all.

Spiritual discipline is like sailing. If the wind represents the grace of God and the distant shore represents our destination (the goal of Christlikeness), then the sail represents spiritual discipline. It catches the grace of God as a sail catches the wind and so moves us toward maturity. Both wind and sail are necessary to get the boat to the other side, but the wind is primary; it is the power. To believe that the hoisting of the sail merited or caused the blowing of the wind would be ludicrous. Likewise, it would be foolish to think that if a person blew into a sail he could propel the boat to the other side. Equally absurd, however, would be the opposite error: to refuse to put up a sail because, after all, nothing but the wind could drive the boat to the other shore anyway. Discipline is necessary, but God's grace is primary. By practicing discipline, we receive and benefit from his grace. Discipline always looks beyond itself, to God and his gifts.

Ends and Means

Spiritual *discipline* and the calling of *discipleship* are not the same thing. Discipleship is the end and discipline, an important means. Progress in discipleship depends on the power of God because our ultimate destiny is simply beyond human attainment. The goal, then, transcends the practice of discipline, although it still requires it.

We must therefore be careful not to equate discipleship with discipline. If we do, we elevate discipline to a position of prominence it should not have. Also, we *reduce* the Christian life to the exercise of discipline and disregard God's comprehensive design for life. This inevitably leads either to despair, if we fail in our efforts to be disciplined, or to pride, if we succeed. Neither are Christian options. Further, excessive dependence on discipline causes us to make it an end in itself. To succeed in it, we tend to develop discipline only where we are already strong and thus build only on our natural inclinations: study will be for the scholar, not the laborer; service for the weak, not the strong; prayer for the mystical, not the practical; silence for the quiet, not the talkative. Our Christian life becomes reoriented so that it becomes *our* discipline, *our* consistency, *our* strengths, *our* efforts.

But once we see that discipline is only a posture we assume to receive grace from God, then we find freedom, freedom to be ourselves, to develop our aptitudes, to face our weaknesses, to try new things. We do not risk ultimate failure. God's at work; we are not alone. We will even dare to develop discipline in areas of personal weakness, where there appears to be no hope of any real achievement. We will no longer have to depend exclusively on that one strength that promises to make us successful, for God promises to give us a greatness that no herculean strength could achieve. Hence the talkative can practice silence; the powerful can pray; the educated can serve; the rich can become poor. Such is the liberty found in spiritual discipline.

Spiritual discipline also differs from obedience (see chapter eighteen). Obedience is the logical response of faith to the commands of

God, and it is possible only if we have already received his grace and acknowledged his goodness. Sometimes obedience leads to failure, loss, even death. Spiritual discipline, on the other hand, is the posture we must assume to receive God's grace. Discipline cultivates a kind of righteous greediness for God; obedience tells the world we are rich with him. Obedience is like the real game: the minutes are ticking away, the points are mounting up, the stakes are getting higher, the pressure is on. Discipline is like the practice session, when there is time for repetition and training. Since God is God, we can breathe in his life—that is discipline. Since God is God, we can exhale his life into the world—that is obedience.

David was *obedient* to God when he heard Goliath taunt the people of Israel. He volunteered to fight because he trusted in God. "Who is this uncircumcised Philistine that he should defy the armies of the living God?" Later he refused to retaliate against King Saul, though he had every right to, because he believed that God would vindicate him. Yet David was also *disciplined*. While still a shepherd he contemplated the character of God. "The Lord is my shepherd, I shall not want." When hiding from Saul in the wilderness he meditated on God.

O God, thou art my God, I seek thee,
   my soul thirsts for thee;
my flesh faints for thee,
   as in a dry and weary land where no water is.
So I have looked upon thee in the sanctuary,
   beholding thy power and glory.
Because thy steadfast love is better than life,
   my lips will praise thee.
So I will bless thee as long as I live;
   I will lift up my hands and call on thy name. (Ps 63:1-4)

Jesus was both perfectly obedient and perfectly disciplined. One moment he was casting out demons, preaching good news, healing the sick, confronting the Pharisees. The next moment he was slipping away quietly to be alone with his Father. He trusted in and acted on God's grace; but he also took time to receive it.

Spiritual discipline moves us in three directions: upward, toward God; inward, toward the body of Christ; outward, toward the world. The following is a brief explanation of each direction and a description of a few of the disciplines themselves.

The Upward Disciplines

The upward disciplines enable us to know God better. The practice of these disciplines makes us aware that God is alive and reigning over the earth. By using them we are enlightened. The apostle Paul talks about the goals of these disciplines when he prays "that the God of our Lord Jesus Christ, the Father of glory, may give you a spirit of wisdom and of revelation in the knowledge of him, *having the eyes of your hearts enlightened*" (Eph 1:17-18).

The Bible teaches that another world, a larger reality, encompasses our own. The upward disciplines enable us to perceive this world and allow it to penetrate our own. Thus we will begin to understand the character of God, the underlying principles governing life, the nature and purpose of the created order and the meaning and direction of history.

1. Study and meditation. Study gives knowledge; meditation gives insight. To study, we should choose a book of the Bible and read it carefully. We should also research the background of the book by consulting a good commentary or Bible dictionary. We need to ask of the text, Why did the author write this? What did he want to tell the people of God? What timeless truths are contained in it? To meditate, we should memorize a passage, or at least become extremely familiar with it; then we should ruminate on it and let it awaken us to truth, using it as a channel to get into the heart of God. Meditation requires silence, passivity, openness, desire, a mind filled with God's Word.

2. Prayer and silence. Prayer is human talk to God. The discipline of prayer includes worship, thanksgiving, confession, praise and petition. The Psalms are useful examples of such prayers. We should memorize some of them and employ them as we pray to God. The prayers of the great saints can also help us to express our deepest longings to God. Silence, on the other hand, makes us listen and allows God to speak. We open our minds, turn off the noise, stop our racing and wait quietly. Other thoughts will intrude; we can expect that. But if we submit them to God and ignore those constant but subtle interruptions, then we will begin to perceive God and let him impart his life and wisdom to us.

The Inward Disciplines

The practice of the inward disciplines purifies and fortifies the church so that God's Spirit can possess it and God's grace direct it. They create a climate in which it is possible to pursue discipleship because the community values it and nurtures it. The inward disciplines thus build an organism, the body of Christ.

1. *Forbearance and correction.* To forbear (Eph 4:1-3) means to tolerate, to put up with, to give slack to. Forbearance in the church makes us teachable, allowing us to recognize that everyone in the body of Christ, however young and immature, has something to contribute, even to the oldest and wisest. Forbearance creates an atmosphere in which people can be themselves and find their own way to maturity. It is best practiced actively, by affirming the good qualities we see in people, and not passively, by merely overlooking faults. Correction, on the other hand, defers to biblical standards for the church (Mt 18:15-18; Gal 6:1). Jesus commands us to go to our brothers and sisters if they have sinned and to admonish and encourage them. This of course requires humility and teachableness.

2. *Roles and gifts.* To fulfill our role we must obey the commands of Christ to the church. No member is exempt. All must serve, witness and encourage. But Christ has also given us special gifts. These are natural affinities which if submitted to the Spirit are supernaturally bridled to build up the church (1 Cor 12:12-26; Rom 12:1-8; Eph 4:1-16). Thus, while all are called to be servants, only some receive the gift of service. While all are commanded to have faith, some have the gift of faith. Gifts add diversity; roles build commonality. Together they create unity.

The Outward Disciplines

The outward disciplines help us to understand both the needs of the world and God's plan to redeem the world. Practicing them makes us discerning and sensitive. Christians should always be the sharpest critics and yet the biggest dreamers, the most critical and the most gracious. To reclaim the world we must learn how to tear down and build up. The outward disciplines will enable us to know when, where and how to do that. Nehemiah's fasting, for example, enabled him to hear God's calling, to follow God's direction and to face the opposition. Jesus' prayer for the world led him to the cross. Our prayers might do the same.

1. *Poverty and worldliness.* The world is a good place. Thus Paul argued that all things are to be received with thanksgiving (1 Tim 4). Jesus was accused of being a glutton and a drunkard because, contrary to the Pharisees, he knew how to enjoy life. The earth was created for our care and pleasure. Christians should celebrate that. Both in nature and in the arts, in all forms of labor and leisure, we should be the leaders in showing the world how to delight in creation without ruining it. But the world is also fallen. Nature is violent and man is vile. Millions are dying of poverty and disease. Jesus commanded us to identify with "the least of these my brethren," in the same way he identified with us. Thus we must learn to live simply and sacrificially even as we live joyfully and abundantly.

2. *Supplication and action.* Supplication is bold and brazen prayer. "Thy will be done on earth as it is in heaven." Praying that way demonstrates humility and courage. We know that human effort alone is vain. The task is too great, the opposition too fierce, the goal too high. So we pray, as Jesus did. Action, on the other hand, shows that we are responsible for the world. We are enjoined to apply Christ's work of redemption to all of life. Where there is injustice, we must challenge; where there is hunger, we must feed; where there is division, we must reconcile. We must act compassionately and pray persistently. That is the balance we need.

Obviously we will not learn to practice all of these disciplines overnight. It will require a lifetime of struggle and application. But as we try—and we must, if we want to receive what God freely gives—we will discover the bounty and beauty of the grace of God. By hoisting our sails, we will catch the wind of God and so be driven to our greater destiny.

Study Questions
1. What are the inherent problems in the following statements?
   a. "I had a terrible day. I knew that would happen once I skipped my morning quiet time."
   b. "This personal piety stuff—Bible reading and prayer—is just producing a private form of Christianity. We need social action, not private expression. Forget a quiet time and obey God for a change."
   c. "I'm getting nothing out of the Bible. And when I pray I don't feel that I'm getting through to God. This spiritual discipline stuff isn't for me. It doesn't work."
2. What do you learn about spiritual discipline from 1 Timothy 4:1-10 and 1 Corinthians 9:24-27?
3. Have you ever tried to be disciplined in some pursuit and failed? Why do some people have trouble with discipline?
4. What are the benefits of defining spiritual discipline as "assuming postures to receive what God wants to give"?
5. Read over the section on exercises again. What specific exercises do you think you need to use? How should you do this? When?

Chapter 18

JOYFUL
OBEDIENCE

Is CHRISTIANITY HARD OR easy?" I asked the Sage one day while we were walking along the beach. "Do you remember the story I told you about the king and his four adopted children?" the Sage asked. "I never told you the end of the story.

"As you might recall, the king was caught in a dilemma. On the one hand, he intended to share the throne with his children, provided they prepare themselves for it adequately. On the other hand, they had shown little regard for his wishes. They wanted the privileges without the responsibilities, and so they refused to submit to the regimented scheme he had designed for them. What was he going to do? The future of his kingdom was at stake, to say nothing of their happiness. He thought about it for several months; finally he devised a plan.

"He summoned them to his royal chambers. With both kindness and severity he told them that life in the castle was going to be different. There would be no more fine dresses, hours of leisure time in the library or fanatical devotion to one cause. He would insist that they follow a strict plan to prepare them for their royal responsibilities. They had two options: obey or leave. Then he addressed each of them individually.

"Henry, the one who loved to study but who spurned exercise and civility, was commanded to practice using the bow and sword for three hours a day. Further, every evening he had to entertain the castle guests and engage them in lively conversation, even if it meant having to be polite, something he hated.

"The king told Elizabeth that she could no longer eat at the great table, except on Sundays. Nor could she wear expensive dresses, eat rich food, drink the best wines or gossip about others. She also had to lose twenty-five pounds. Moreover, she was to rise every morning at 6:00 A.M. for exercise and study. She shuddered at the thought of it. 'Early' to her had been 10:00 A.M.

"Jonathan was ordered to stay *inside* the castle except for two hours a day, when he was allowed to practice in the fields. While inside, he was to read, do domestic chores and meet with the captains of the army to plan for *real* battles and conquests. In four months he would be sent north on an expedition to search for the treasures of the great dragon.

"Finally, Sarah was not allowed to leave the castle grounds at all. 'No more noble causes for you, fair lady,' he said to her. 'Not for a while at least.' Instead, the king commanded her to live an ordinary life, until she learned to think before she acted.

"Each adopted orphan, in other words, was directed to do the very thing necessary to make them truly royal. The king's commands, however severe they appeared to be, were an expression of his love and dreams for them.

"It was hard for all of them. Not that the regimentation itself was difficult, because it wasn't. But since they had become so lopsided in their interests it was painful for them to become well-rounded again. Not all of them cooperated.

"Sarah stayed in the castle for a month, but she never adjusted to a common way of life, nor did she bridle her striving spirit. One day she fled. She had heard about a war in the east and wanted to fight in it. She was, however, woefully unprepared and uninformed. She joined the wrong side, fought in the wrong battle and was eventually betrayed and murdered by the very people she wanted to help. Henry resisted too. He considered practice and politeness to be a waste of time, far beneath a person of his intellectual acumen. He left the castle and enrolled in a university where he earned a degree in magic. One day he used the wrong potion in an experiment and vanished. Sadly, he had become so snobbish that no one missed him except the kind old king.

"Only Jonathan and Elizabeth obeyed the king's commands. Eventually Elizabeth became a famous woman, renowned for her modesty, discipline and charity. She also became a gracious host and a servant to the poor. Jonathan traveled to the north, as he was ordered to, although he dreaded the mission and thought himself to be unprepared. He succeeded, much to his surprise, and returned to the castle a hero. In time he also learned the value of leisure. He became not only a great knight but also a famous spinner of tales. The king invited both of them to share his throne, and after his death each of them received half the kingdom as an inheritance."

"But you haven't answered my question," I said after he finished the story. "Is the Christian faith hard or easy?"

"What do you think?"

"Right now it seems hard," I said. "Will it ever get easy?"

"I hope so. And yes, I also think so. I believe we were created to be obedient. It's true to our nature."

"But why, then, is disobedience so natural to me?"

"Because it has become natural, too, but in a different, more superficial way. It's getting from one state to the other that's awkward and, well, very hard at times. Sometimes I wonder whether I'm making any progress at all."

"I suppose it's all a matter of time and patience," I said.

"And obedience," the Sage replied.

*   *   *

Obedience, Obligation and God

Does obedience deprive us of true freedom? Many people think so, thus betraying a negative view of obedience. We see obedience as giving God his due, and happiness as what is left over for ourselves. Obedience is viewed as an *obligation*. Suppose, for example, that we had invited God into our home as a special guest; we might let him have the run of it, except for one room. That little room would represent our desire to withhold just a little from God so that we could keep something all for ourselves.

Such an attitude implies that God is not really capable or willing to give us the best in life. Further, it implies that happiness is largely the result of human effort and not a divine gift. Finally, it suggests that it is possible to withhold something of ourselves from God, as if God could be satisfied owning just a part of us. We are wrong on all three counts.

Obedience is the logical response to three indisputable facts: God is sovereign, having the ability to give us the best; God is good, desiring to give us the best; God is wise, knowing what that best is and telling us so in the Bible. Obedience enables us to live in harmony with these facts; disobedience challenges them and so leads to death. That is why rebellious people are always being broken by their own disobedience. It is hard to defy absolute laws, like gravity, and succeed. Obedience, then, cannot be conceived of as a list of impossible and impractical commands meant to be followed only by the few Christians who are masochistic enough to live miserably. Christlike living is logical, natural living, once we acknowledge the true facts about life.

Obedience is an investment in absolute reality. It is a way of affirming that God is true and trustworthy and that he has designed life to be lived a certain way. As God's existence is written right into the nature of things, so are the principles he established for living. In fact, God and his law are inextricably bound up together. Common sense, therefore, should make us obey, for obedience is the way of investing in what is ultimately true about life. "Do not lay up for yourselves treasures on earth, where moth and rust consume and where thieves break in and steal, but lay up for yourselves treasures in heaven, where neither moth nor rust consumes and where thieves do not break in and steal. For where your treasure is, there will your heart be also" (Mt 6:19-21).

That is why Jesus was so firm about the law. He knew that because the law is a reflection of God's goodness, sovereignty and wisdom, it was absolutely true and unchanging; it corresponded to the way God designed life to be lived under his authority. Hence he argued that it was impossible for us to break the law without also breaking ourselves.

> Think not that I have come to abolish the law and the prophets; I have come not to abolish them but to fulfil them. For truly, I say to you, till heaven and earth pass away, not an iota, not a dot, will pass from the law until all is accomplished. Whoever then relaxes one of the least of these commandments and teaches men so, shall be called least in the kingdom of heaven; but he who does them and teaches them shall be called great in the kingdom of heaven. For I tell you, unless your righteousness exceeds that of the scribes and Pharisees, you will never enter the kingdom of heaven. (Mt 5:17-20)

Jesus preached the Sermon on the Mount to clarify the real intent of the law. "You have heard that it was said . . . but I say to you . . ." He argued that the laws of God are not accidentally connected to life. They are written into the very nature of things. They are divine principles which, if followed, will *eventually* make life prosperous and, if violated, will eventually make life miserable. They link us harmoniously with ultimate reality. In other words, "don't jump off the cliff" is a good warning if gravity exists. "Don't play with matches" is a good rule if fire burns. "Don't slander your brother or sister" is a good law if our words will acquit or condemn us for all eternity (Mt 12:33-36). "Love your neighbor as yourself" is a good principle if love is at the very foundation of our world. "Seek first his kingdom" is a good command if there is a kingdom worth seeking (Mt 6:33). These are not only good laws; they are necessary ones. Obedience is more than a matter of obligation; it is a matter of logic.

We were created to be obedient. Once we overcome our evil bent and begin to live obediently, we will also find ourselves living more naturally. E. Stanley Jones writes:

> The universe is not indifferent to your virtue and your vice; it takes sides. It is a universe where you get results or consequences. If you work with the moral universe, you get results; it will back you, sustain you, and further you; you will have cosmic backing for your way of life. You will get results. But if you go against the moral universe, you get consequences; you will be up against reality; you will be frustrated. Some people go through life getting results. Others get consequences. You are free to choose, but you are not free to choose the results or the consequences of your choices; they are in hands not your own. You do not break these laws written into the nature of things; you break yourselves on them. These laws are class-blind, color-blind, race-blind, religion-blind; break them and you get broken.[28]

The Road of Faith

To obey God, we must learn to view life through the eyes of faith. "And without faith it is impossible to please him. For whoever would draw near to God must believe that he exists and that he rewards those who seek him. . . . By faith Abraham obeyed" (Heb 11:6, 8). Faith enables us to see life from a larger frame of reference. Faith is necessary because, at least initially, obedience is painful. That was what finally separated the four children in the Sage's story. Jonathan and Elizabeth saw what could be, should they be obedient. They endured the pain of obedience and so received the inheritance. Sarah and Henry, on the other hand, were tyrannized by the immediate and so never conquered what kept them from following the king's commands.

Jesus warned us about the wide gate and easy road that leads to destruction (Mt 7:13-14). Faith gives us the perspective to counter the false logic of the world and to dare to take the road least traveled, the narrow and hard one leading to life. Faith gives us the capacity to endure when obedience breaks us of those unnatural affections that have become natural to us. Without faith, then, radical obedience will be impossible; in fact, the very idea of it will repulse us. The Bible will appear to command us to do painful, insane things. Noah was called crazy by his contemporaries when he began building an ark in the middle of a desert, but not after it started to rain. As it turned out, the people were crazy for mocking and not helping him. Moses was considered a fool to abandon his prestigious position in Egypt to identify with a nation of slaves— that is, until the Red Sea parted. Esther was insane to risk her life for the sake of her Jewish brethren, especially with Haman, hungry for power and thirsty for blood, lurking about. But who had the final word?

Every command of God is related to his sovereignty, goodness and wisdom. Every act of obedience, therefore, is a way of affirming our trust in him. We cannot obey God if we do not believe that he is truly God. Hence Paul used the phrase "the obedience of faith" (Rom 1:5; Gal 5:6). If God is God, obedience makes sense; if he is not, it is insane. For example, consider God's command to husbands: "Love your wives, as Christ loved the church" (Eph 5:25). Such love must be sacrificial, consistent, dogged. Few men will obey this command unless they trust in the goodness of God. Professional aspirations, the encroachment of old age and the pressures of culture will cause them to use rather than serve their wives and to neglect rather than cherish them. Only faith can persuade husbands to believe that obedience leads to the best in life when it requires them to give so much up.

A Logical and Wonderful Requirement

The author of Hebrews says that it is impossible to obey unless we first have faith. But the book of James says that faith *necessarily* leads to obedience (Jas 2). The two are inseparable. One cannot be a

Christian and not obey.

Either we believe that God is the center of the universe, or we do not. None of us can tolerate holding both views at the same time. What is important in our discussion here is not obedience itself but the world view that inspires it. True faith engenders allegiance to a divine master. Consider, for example, the words of Jesus, "No one can serve two masters; for either he will hate the one and love the other, or he will be devoted to the one and despise the other" (Mt 6:24). Paul expands on this point, "But I say, walk by the Spirit, and do not gratify the desires of the flesh. For the desires of the flesh are against the Spirit, and the desires of the Spirit are against the flesh; for these are opposed to each other, to prevent you from doing what you would" (Gal 5:16-17).

Jesus and Paul taught twin truths. We have the option of serving *one* of two masters—the flesh or the spirit, the way of man or the way of God, self-rule or divine rule. Paul wrote that these are *opposed* to each other; they are mutually exclusive. What we would like is to have the best of both worlds: the benefits of knowing God *and* the immediate pleasures of serving the self. That is something we cannot have.

What happens when we try? "The eye is the lamp of the body. So, if your eye is sound, your whole body will be full of light; but if your eye is not sound, your whole body will be full of darkness. If then the light *in* you is darkness, how great is the darkness!" (Mt 6:22-23). The vain attempt to serve two masters causes spiritual blindness. It is like trying to be married to two equally demanding people or trying to serve two equally exacting employers. It is only a matter of time before we are found out. In the meantime we delude ourselves into thinking we can fool both of them. In the end we only fool ourselves.

Double-mindedness drives us to God one moment and away from him the next, thus depriving us of the benefits of purity, on the one hand, and the pleasures of sin, on the other. This pattern of leaving God and returning to God happens so repeatedly that after a time we begin to doubt our own religious sincerity and project this onto

God. "How can God forgive me again?" we say to ourselves. But what we really mean is, "How can I presume to ask him to forgive me anymore?" Hebrews 6 tells us that none of us can be restored to grace if we willfully persist in disobeying God, not because God will not forgive but because we can no longer repent. When we reject the rigors but not the advantages of discipleship and refuse to submit to the Christian view of reality, we become blinded by our own double-mindedness. *Our* hearts become hardened toward God, not God's heart toward us. If we refuse to be obedient and still try to be Christian, we play with fire. In the end we only delude ourselves.

A Violent Peace

Now we can understand the price of obedience. Jesus said, "The law and the prophets were until John; since then the good news of the kingdom of God is preached, and every one enters it violently" (Lk 16:16). Neither the Gospels nor the book of Acts describes placid entries into the kingdom. Peter's agony during Christ's last days exposed his self-interest and hunger for power. He wanted immediate fame; Jesus promised suffering. Obedience was a tumultuous ordeal for Peter. It will be for us, too. While it eventually leads to a natural and wonderful way of life—the one for which we were created—its initial impact brings pain. In this sense it is like birth, which is both violent and miraculous, full of agony and joy.

In fact, Jesus warned us about the pain of obedience even when he was promising us ultimate gain. He said there would be losses. He taught that we must lose our lives to gain them, renounce what we have to inherit the world, and become servants of all to follow him in his exaltation.

Paul, too, wrote that we are "heirs of God and fellow heirs with Christ, provided we suffer with him in order that we may also be glorified with him" (Rom 8:17). At another point he wrote, "This slight momentary affliction is preparing for us an eternal weight of glory beyond all comparison, because we look not to the things that are seen but to the things that are unseen; for the things that are seen are transient, but the things that are unseen are eternal" (2 Cor 4:17-18).

At first obedience seems to work against us rather than for us. In the long run, however, a little obedience opens the way to an exponential burst of gain; and disobedience, while initially posing no problem, plunges us into ruin. The ultimate difference between the two is extreme, as extreme as the difference between heaven and hell. "Let us fix our eyes on Jesus," the author of Hebrews says, "who for the joy set before him endured the cross" (12:2). Like Noah, Abraham, Moses, Esther and the others who went before him, Jesus set his sights on ultimate reality, the kingdom of God. He believed that God, his Father, was good, sovereign and wise; so he lived accordingly. We are called to that same kind of complete obedience (see Heb 11), even when, with Jesus, we must suffer because of it.

Natural or Unnatural?

We have seen that obedience is really natural to us. But then so is sin. What is the difference?

Sin is natural to sinners in the same way, for example, that alcoholism is natural to alcoholics. Drunkenness is natural because they feel at home in it, and soberness and eventual abstinence are unnatural because they seem foreign. Their bodies crave the bottle. To be broken of this is extremely hard. Yet their bodies were made for sobriety, not alcohol. Their minds *really* crave clarity, not cloudiness. If they can overcome their alcoholism, an admittedly difficult task, they will live in a way that is natural—right and true—to their whole being, and drunkenness will be shown to be an invader and a parasite of their true selves.

In the same way our real selves desire to obey God. Once we learn obedience, a tough task, we will for the first time find ourselves swimming with and not against the current of our whole being and the entire universe. It will be as natural as God is real, as easy as God is good. We were made for obedience. Nothing less will really do.

Study Questions

1. How do you respond to the charge that Christianity is too demanding, that it is unrealistic in all that it asks of a person?

2. According to Hebrews 11, what role does faith play in obedience?

3. In Matthew 5:10 Jesus says, "Blessed are those who are persecuted for righteousness' sake, for theirs is the kingdom of heaven." How are we to view the suffering we experience when we are being obedient?

4. How must you change your view of reality in order to make it compatible with God's summons to obedience? How should you obey God now?

Chapter 19

EMBRACING
THE WHOLE

IT WAS THE MIDDLE OF August. Since my dad was planning for us to drive home the following Sunday to give him time to prepare for another school year, the whole family decided we should have one last gathering to end the summer on a high note. I suggested we hold a great feast, and they all agreed. My mother said the Sage should be included, too. He had become such a close friend of all of us that we felt we weren't quite a family without him. I was sent to invite him for that night.

When I walked into his cabin I found him talking on the phone. He waved me over and pointed to a letter lying on top of the desk. Motioning with his lips, he told me to read it. It said the following:

William,

I have sad news for you. Frank Niebolt, the lawyer who handled our international affairs, died of liver cancer last week. We found out about the cancer only five weeks ago. He deteriorated very quickly. The funeral was one of the more moving I have ever attended. The presiding pastor talked about the hope of the resurrection, and his oldest son gave a testimony which pointed to the power of God in his dad's life. We shall miss him.

You know I have mentioned this to you before. Nevertheless, I feel compelled to do it again. We need your services here at Global Action, especially with Frank now gone. You have the expertise, heart and vision we need. I realize that you are writing a book. Can you postpone it for a while, or work on it in conjunction with your work here? Consider my invitation carefully. We will pray for you here. I'll call you in a few days. . . .

"All right, Ed, thanks for calling. I'll write you in a week or two. . . . Call? . . . In two days? . . . Patience, my friend. I need time to think about this."

The Sage hung up the phone and laughed.

"The same man who wrote the letter?" I inquired.

"The same man," the Sage said. "Did you read it?"

"Sounds like he really wants you," I said. "Will you go?"

"I don't know," he replied. "I suppose so. It's a surprise, really. I had no idea that Frank was that sick."

"Did you know him?"

"Not really. I met him once or twice. But I know Ed very well. He used to live in New York City."

"What about your book?"

"I just completed the rough draft. I need to let it sit awhile— perhaps five or six months—before I revise it. But *I* can't sit that long. I've been thinking about moving for a few weeks now."

"Back to New York?"

"Yes, until I got this offer from Global Action, which is located in California."

"What's 'Global Action'?"

"A Christian organization founded to relieve suffering in the world. It's an impressive one. I'd feel honored to serve in it. But what a change it would be!"

"You mean from living here, in Michigan?"

"No, I was thinking of the contrast between Global Action and the Public Defender's Office in New York. I can't imagine working with all Christians. It scares me a little."

"Why?"

"Too easy to get self-satisfied. Still, I guess it doesn't really matter where I live or work. In fact, this might be good preparation since the kingdom will eventually encompass everything anyway. It will conquer."

"You make it sound like we're in a war," I said.

"We *are* in a war," the Sage said, "between good and evil, heaven and hell, light and darkness. And this planet of ours is the battlefield and the prize. I like what C. S. Lewis wrote, 'All that seems earth is either hell or heaven.' The earth is like one big womb that is giving birth, very violently, to creatures and cultures that will be either parts of hell or heaven. What we do now moves us closer to one or the other."

"That makes me feel a little nervous," I said.

"Me, too," he said. "One thing always leads to another. There's no neutrality. Either we're being conquered by and prepared for life in the kingdom of God, or we're being conquered by and prepared for life in hell."

"But it doesn't seem like the kingdom is conquering anything," I objected. "I mean, look at your friend who just died of cancer."

"Sometimes I feel the same way. Evil *is* powerful. It doesn't respect neutral borders any more than cancer does. Like cancer, evil can't help but grow."

"So what's the use?"

"Because the kingdom can't help but expand either. It's like light. Switch on a light in a darkened room. What happens? Darkness is dispelled because it's no match for light's greater power. I believe—in fact, I know—that the kingdom will conquer this world of ours. God is Ruler; Satan is only a usurper. Good will triumph."

"Everywhere?"

"Everywhere except hell. The conflict is the same and the outcome is certain no matter where you live or what you do. The kingdom will conquer at the Public Defender's Office and at Global Action, just in different ways."

"Even at college," I said.

"Yes, even at college. Do you believe it?"

"Yes, I think I do. I can't wait to get there. I'm excited about what can happen."

Then I looked at the Sage. "When will you be leaving?"

"Not for a while," the Sage said. "Shall we go down to the beach?"

We walked out of his cabin. It was a wonderful morning; one of the finest of the summer. When we got down to the beach we headed south, toward our cottage. I felt alive and aware of everything—the warm air, the chattering shoreline, the cool sand in my toes, the canopy of blue over my head. I knew right then that the God of the kingdom had laid claim to me. And I also knew that he was somehow going to lay claim to the world around me.

*   *   *

Reclaiming Our World

We are not wanting these days for worthy causes. For example, I receive an average of ten letters a week from organizations that ask, and sometimes beg, for my support. That is over forty pieces of mail a month, five hundred a year. I am battered by their appeals. If I were to respond to them all, I would save whales, ban handguns, fight abortion, blast rock music, march on Washington, lobby Congress, feed the hungry, dismantle the nuclear arsenal, preserve important buildings, protect our soil and forests, cut the budget, censor books, censor the censors, evangelize Europe, help refugees, visit prisons, reclaim college campuses, get moral, tolerate diversity . . .

Not that these causes are trivial. To the contrary, many of them prick my conscience and break my heart. When I read these letters (all of them written so carefully and often underlined with blue ink and touched up with handwritten notes), I am moved to want to help the suffering victims of the world, those dying, dead or hell-bound people whose needs would have been overlooked had not some organization taken up their cause. But if I did, I would have to file for bankruptcy within a month and enter a hospital for a nervous breakdown. There seem to be just too many good causes.

Still, there is a positive side to this proliferation. Mainstream Christianity is being awakened to the needs of the world. Christians are recognizing the logical implications of the gospel. We are learning that its message is addressed to real people—the starving, the oppressed, the wealthy, the secular—who live in a complicated society—democratic, socialist, totalitarian—which faces serious problems—violence, abortion, injustice. We have discovered the meaning of the Incarnation, Christ's bold, reckless identification with sinful humanity. We want to follow his example. Some have even started to and are seeing that the gospel speaks to the whole of humanity and to the whole of society—hence the explosion of those organizations and causes. We all know, in general terms, what must be done. Now we need to understand how God will help us get it done.

God is committed to reclaim the earth for his kingdom. He is not only the Redeemer of the world, but he is also its Creator. The world, therefore, rightfully belongs to him, twice over. He made it; and he sent Jesus to pay an infinite price to buy it back. In fact, creation sets the stage for redemption. God made the world for us. When we rebelled, the whole world was affected. All of creation toppled into corruption with our Fall, as Paul argues in Romans 8. Thus, when God extends his grace to us, he embraces us in our environment and social setting. He purposes to reclaim the whole world. Souls are not saved; people are. Individuals are not the only entities reached; so are communities. Our problems are straightened out, yes; but so are the social contexts in which we live. God has never nullified his original purpose; he will not abandon the "good" world he created, however corrupted it has become.

But we are still responsible. Right from the beginning God intended us to be custodians of this planet and vicegerents of his kingdom; and he did not change his mind after the Fall. The Bible says that we were created not only *in* God's likeness but also *for* creative dominion. We are answerable to God for the world he made and entrusted to our care, regardless of (and, in a sense, because of) the devastating consequences of the Fall. When God restores to us our relationship with him, he also restores to us our responsibility for the world. We cannot cleave faith from work. God will not allow it. He has given us many examples to point the way. Joseph, Daniel and Esther brought their faith to bear on the political arena. Amos did not tolerate the convenient division between religion and daily life made by the people of his day.

I hate, I despise your feasts,
and I take no delight in your solemn assemblies.
Even though you offer me your burnt offerings and cereal offerings,
I will not accept them. . . .
Take away from me the noise of your songs;
to the melody of your harps I will not listen.
But let justice roll down like waters,
and righteousness like an everflowing stream. (Amos 5:21-24)

Two hundred years ago William Carey, the father of the modern Protestant missionary movement, appealed to the Church of England to send him to India. They refused. "If God wants to save the heathen then he will do it, without our help." They were dangerously mistaken. Jesus said, "Go!" God asked Isaiah, "Whom will I send, and who will go for me?" Ezekiel could find no one to "stand in the gap and build up the wall." The world is our responsibility. It was made for us; now it must be reclaimed by us. As the Sage intimated, we are in a war.

Weakness and Prayer

Yet the task is larger and the enemy greater than human power is able to handle. We are engaged in a spiritual conflict, largely invisible, whose effects are, nevertheless, horribly visible. The holocaust and other historical tragedies are the work of people twisted by the demonic. Evil has more than a foothold in our world; it has an extensive kingdom ruled by a vicious king. "Our fight is not against flesh and blood," Paul said. The entire New Testament narrative assumes the existence of Satanic forces. We cannot understand the ministry of Christ and the church without identifying the principal antagonist. Jesus came not only to reclaim human life and society but also to wage war against a demonic dominion. He showed that heaven and hell are fighting a fierce battle. "This world is both the battlefield and the prize," the Sage said.

Jesus wrestled with Satan throughout his life. Just after Christ's birth Satan almost succeeded in having him murdered by King Herod. After his baptism he was tempted by the devil. During his public ministry Jesus plundered the house of Satan; the deeds of his disciples, he said, made Satan fall like lightning from heaven. The crucifixion was orchestrated not simply by the Jews and Romans but also by the principalities and powers. In many of his letters Paul mentions the powers of darkness. We are also warned by Peter to beware of our foe, who wanders about like a roaring lion seeking to devour its prey. This is brutal business.

We are responsible for the world, a world engulfed by conflict. But the combat requires a power only God can provide. We are thus commanded to use the resources of heaven and pray earnestly for God's help. Human ingenuity and organizations are not enough. They indicate our good intentions, but they also expose our presumptuousness. We cannot succeed without God; but he has chosen only to act through us. So in our earthen vessels we are to act in faith, depending on divine power (2 Cor 4:7-12).

Thus we pray, "Thy kingdom come." The corporate prayers of the church are a weapon largely overlooked by Christians. Many of us have tried hard to live out our Christian convictions but have disregarded the basic world view that directed the life of the early church. That is as foolish as trying to launch a satellite without referring to the theories of Einstein. Serious prayer, informed by a biblical cosmology, unleashes the powers of heaven, drives back the forces of hell and ignites the church to fruitful action. It prepares the way for our radical work in the world. Prayer, then, must become our passion.

After Peter and John were released from prison they gathered together with the other disciples and told them what had happened. Then, instead of running from the conflict or bemoaning their circumstances, they prayed:

> Sovereign Lord, who didst make the heaven and the earth and the sea and everything in them, who by the mouth of our father David, thy servant, didst say by the Holy Spirit, "Why did the Gentiles rage, and the people imagine vain things? The kings of the earth set themselves in array, and the rulers were gathered together, against the Lord and against his Anointed"—for truly in this city there were gathered together against thy holy servant Jesus, whom thou didst anoint, both Herod and Pontius Pilate, with the Gentiles and the peoples of Israel, to do whatever thy hand and thy plan predestined to take place. And now, Lord, look upon their threats, and grant to thy servants to speak thy word with all boldness, while thou stretchest out thy hand to heal, and signs and wonders are performed through the name of thy holy servant Jesus. (Acts 4:24-30)

Luke adds that the place in which they were praying was shaken. They were filled with the Holy Spirit and spoke the Word with boldness. Why? Because they were fighting the real enemy in a real war using real weapons. And we are the beneficiaries of their obedience. Will future generations extol our example as we do the early church's? We shall answer that question largely on our knees.

A Kingdom Commission

Jesus' own public ministry points the way for us. Jesus used the phrase *the kingdom of God* to show how expansive is God's scheme for the world. "The time is fulfilled, and the kingdom of God is at hand; repent, and believe in the gospel" (Mk 1:15). The kingdom of God was the driving force in Jesus' ministry. He was considered a threat to the religious, legal and political establishment because he was a King with a universal kingdom. It was not *of* this world, as Jesus said; but it was certainly *for* this world and *against* its evil practices. Likewise, the early church disrupted certain segments of the economic order because it, too, preached the Christ of the kingdom (Acts 13, 16, 19).

We have tended to favor weaker, truncated terms: *evangelism, social witness* and the like. These have become divisive and misleading because they have been disconnected from the larger, more inclusive concept of the kingdom. We evangelize souls or we meet people's physical needs; and so we treat the world as if it were made up of ghosts or living corpses. Only the theology of the kingdom will cause us to mend broken people and thus build a healthy world. It will never allow us to care for farmers and neglect their land, to save the rich and disregard their wealth, to reach the artist and ignore culture, to love the poor and overlook their oppression. The soul and the body constitute one person; the individual and his environment are largely inseparable. And they are all to be transformed by the kingdom.

Thus Jesus has commissioned us not merely to evangelize the lost or erect new church buildings or do social action, but to *make disciples*, a task that matches kingdom theology. A disciple is a learner, a follower, a doer. Cults make disciples; communists make disciples; business enterprises make disciples. That is why they wield such influence. More often than not, Christians make converts or perhaps church members. That is why we falter. Disciples submit their beings to God; converts submit only their hearts. Disciples entrust their time to God; church members give a few hours a week. Jesus commanded us to make disciples (Mt 28:18-20).

This requires that we build a strong church, for Jesus intended the church to create an atmosphere that would make discipleship palatable, concrete, attractive. "They will know you are Christians by how you love one another." The church must become the organism through which God's kingdom is established—not the government or the schools, however important these are. Yes, the church should speak prophetically to the nations. But it should be able to point to itself as an example of what nations and all other structures can and ought to do. The church should be the radical alternative that the larger society is longing to see, and follow. It will lead best by what it does, not merely by what it says; by its suffering, not merely by its resolutions. While governments can pass laws and so create moral boundaries, the church can change lives and so provide a whole new moral direction. The church, then, must be the model of what we want society to be.

A Certain Hope

The kingdom of God is reality; all else is shadow. It will someday rule visibly and completely over the entire universe. Nothing, ultimately, will escape its authority and judgment, not even the deepest crevices and caves in hell. God champions a universal cause; he leads the indomitable armies of heaven. The kingdom of God is ever expanding.

Why? First, because good is greater than evil. While evil is a perversion of good, an ugly parasite that feeds on goodness, good is absolute because it represents the character of God. Since God is sovereign, good will inevitably conquer evil. The Sage argued that good functions like light. If a light is turned on, darkness is dispelled because it is no match for light's greater power. The light of the kingdom will someday shine forth brilliantly at the return of Christ, and the darkness on earth will be exposed and banished to hell. Yet even now, before his return, good pushes evil back. Evil is counting its last days. That is why Satan, his hosts and all the godless are putting up a fierce, albeit futile, attempt to survive before they are sentenced to hell. Good will triumph.

Further, the kingdom of God inevitably expands because it is true to the very nature of reality. It enables things to find and fit the function they were made for. It makes everything work naturally, in the way God intended it to work. Humans were created to live for God, not themselves. The world was created to manifest God's glory, not reflect Satan's ugliness. Though we are free to challenge God's design, to adopt and adapt to inferior and self-destructive patterns of living, we will never learn to live naturally until we return to God; neither will the world, unless we submit it to God. The kingdom is true to the way things were meant to be.

Also, the inevitable expansion of the kingdom follows logically from the lordship of Christ. Paul writes about Jesus:

He is the image of the invisible God, the firstborn of all creation; for in him all things were created, in heaven and on earth, visible and invisible, whether thrones or dominions or principalities or authorities—all things were created through him and for him. He is before all things, and in him all things hold together. He is the head of the body, the church; he is the beginning, the firstborn from the dead, that in everything he might be preeminent. For in him all the fulness of God was pleased to dwell, and through him to reconcile to himself *all things,* whether on earth or in heaven, making peace by the blood of his cross. (Col 1:15-20)

Everything originated in Jesus; and everything finds its purpose in him, because he is Lord. He is the King who has come to claim his kingdom. Though the world has been usurped by evil powers, Christ will not allow it to be divided or ruined. He wants what belongs to him, all of it. It follows that both mind and heart belong to God, pro football as well as church volleyball, talent as much as our trials, culture and church alike.

The kingdom of God will expand—into all parts of us, into all parts of the world. It will triumph. At the beginning of the book we explored the concept of God's loyalty. We end now where we began. As it turns out, God is radically loyal not only to us but also to the whole world. He created it; now he is redeeming it. Incredibly, he has summoned us to participate in that redemptive process. As we were conquered *by* him, so we must now conquer *for* him. We must reclaim the world for the kingdom. That is the inevitable direction discipleship takes. One thing *will* lead to another until all is finished and then submitted, in perfection, before the throne of God.

Then I saw a new heaven and a new earth; for the first heaven and the first earth had passed away, and the sea was no more. And I saw the holy city, new Jerusalem, coming down out of heaven from God, prepared as a bride adorned for her husband; and I heard a loud voice from the throne saying, "Behold, the dwelling of God is with men. He will dwell with them, and they shall be his people, and God himself will be with them; he will wipe away every tear from their eyes, and death shall be no more, neither shall there be mourning nor crying nor pain any more, for the former things have passed away." (Rev 21:1-4)

Study Questions
1. Make a list of all the popular Christian movements and causes you know of. How does each reflect a part of the kingdom of God?
2. What do you think God wants to do with this world of ours? What is our role in this scheme?
3. What do we learn from 2 Corinthians 4:7-12 about the relation between God's power and our weakness?
4. What is our commission according to Luke 4:16-21 and Matthew 28:18-20?
5. How does our task of reclaiming the world for the kingdom affect our view of occupations, social structures, the church, relationships and global problems (for example, world hunger)?
6. In what ways do you need to change your life so that it better reflects the work of the kingdom?

Notes

[1]Lynnell Mickelsen, "The Edge of Hell," *Campus Life Magazine*, May 1980, p. 74.

[2]Howard Taylor, *Hudson Taylor's Spiritual Secret* (Chicago: Moody Press, 1932), pp. 158-59.

[3]Ibid., p. 161.

[4]Isaac Watts, "When I Survey the Wondrous Cross."

[5]Thomas O. Chisholm, "Great Is Thy Faithfulness," © 1923, 1951, Hope Publishing Co.

[6]Walter Chalmers Smith, "Immortal, Invisible, God Only Wise."

[7]Quoted in Hendrikus Berkof, *Christian Faith* (Grand Rapids, Mich.: Eerdmans, 1979), p. 108.

[8]Thomas Merton, *New Seeds of Contemplation* (New York: New Directions, 1961), p. 206.

[9]Carlo Carretto, *Letters from the Desert* (Maryknoll, N.Y.: Orbis Books, 1972).

[10]Henri Nouwen, *Reaching Out* (Garden City, N.Y.: Doubleday, 1975), p. 53.

[11]C. S. Lewis, *Mere Christianity* (New York: Macmillan, 1943), pp. 172-73.

[12]Ibid., pp. 189-90.

[13]Charles Wesley, "Love Divine, All Loves Excelling."

[14]Martin Luther King, Jr., "I Have a Dream," *A Treasury of the World's Great Speeches*, ed. Houston Peterson (New York: Simon and Schuster, 1965), p. 839.

[15]Merton, *New Seeds*, p. 150.

[16]I am indebted to the thinking of Jonathan Edwards, C. S. Lewis and Daniel Fuller in this brief section of the chapter.

[17]Lewis, *Mere Christianity*, p. 142.

[18]Merton, *New Seeds*, pp. 257-58.

[19]E. Stanley Jones, *A Song of Ascents* (New York: Abingdon, 1968), p. 180.

[20]Stuart Babbage, "Lord Kenneth Clark's Encounter with the 'Motions of

Grace,' " *Christianity Today*, 8 June 1979, p. 28.

[21]Peter Kreeft, *Heaven, The Heart's Deepest Longing* (San Francisco: Harper & Row, 1980), pp. 108-9.

[22]Henry Fairlie, *The Seven Deadly Sins Today* (Notre Dame, Ind.: Univ. of Notre Dame Press, 1979).

[23]Lewis, *Mere Christianity*, pp. 109-110.

[24]Merton, *New Seeds*, pp. 38, 42-43, 99.

[25]Ibid., pp. 24-25.

[26]Thomas Kelly, *A Testament of Devotion* (New York: Harper & Row, 1941), pp. 95-96.

[27]Hugh Prather, *Notes to Myself* (New York: Bantam, 1970), p. 10.

[28]Jones, *A Song of Ascents*, pp. 374-75.